INVEST LIKE A PRO

Using Technical Analysis in Multiple Time Frames and Trend Analysis to Improve Timing in Stock Investing

Joe Rabil

Copyright © 2019 by Joe Rabil. 2nd edition. All rights reserved. No part of this publication may be reproduced, stored in a retrieval system, or transmitted in any form or by any means, electronic, mechanical, photocopying, recording, scanning, or otherwise, except as permitted under Section 107 or 108 of the 1976 United States Copyright Act, without the prior written permission of the author.

This book is created for educational purposes only. In no way is this book intended to provide all the answers for successful investing. Investing entails significant risks and should be undertaken only with money that you are comfortable losing. Investing can result in the loss of all the capital that you are using to trade. Successful investing takes a long time to develop and requires experiencing loss on a regular basis. If you use margin to trade, it is possible that you will lose more capital than you have, resulting in large and uncontrollable debt. In no way whatsoever does the author or the publisher assume any liability or responsibility for losses experienced from applying the lessons taught in this book. They cannot and do not assure you of any success in investing as a result of reading the contents of this book. Any investing that you do before or after reading this book is at your own risk.

TABLE OF CONTENTS

Introduction: Invest Like a Pro	7
Why Technical Analysis is Needed	10
A Chart is a Chart	16
100 Bars on a Chart	19
Trend	23
Definitions for a Change in Trend	33
Rules for Multiple Time Frames	43
Incorporating Moving Averages	51
Sample Charts	63
Using the MACD Indicator in Conjunction With the Moving Average Signals	79
Zero Line Reversals	82
Pinch Plays	87
Momentum Divergence	90
Reverse Divergence	96
When to Use the Crossover vs the Pinch	99

Putting It Together: Multiple Time Frames and MACD	101
Using the ADX Indicator	104
ADX is Non-Directional	108
ADX Conditions That Help in Stock Selection	110
More ADX Examples	120
Trading Tactics	124
Trading Plan for the 2-Time Frame Pinch	128
Why Trading is So Difficult – the Math	157
Streaks	159
More Examples to Study	162
Conclusion	169

"The most money is made by swing trading, or in long pull trades, that is following a definite trend as long as the trend is up or down, but you must learn by rules to wait until the market gets out of a rut or a trading range."

"Wait for definite indications that it is going higher or lower, before you take a position for a long pull trade."
– WD GANN 1942

Acknowledgements

I would like to mention some great investors and teachers whose work has had a great influence on me: W.D. Gann, Linda Raschke, Scot Lowry, Dave Landry, Don Miller, Victor Sperandeo, Charles Schaap, Art Merrill, Stan Weinstein, Martin Zweig, and Gerald Appel. These individuals have had success as investors but were also willing to take the time to publish their techniques so others could learn and benefit, and I am grateful for that.

In addition, I would like to thank my longtime business partner, Kevin Howard. We have spent years discussing market movement and formulating strategies together. He was instrumental in helping me to refine and edit the content to make sure the proper meaning came across. I appreciate his perspective and his invaluable assistance.

INTRODUCTION - INVEST LIKE A PRO

The most important thing to learn from this manual is that the techniques professional day traders have used to make money day in and day out for the past few decades will work for longer term investing as well. I will show numerous examples in the coming pages which will help the average investor understand how to apply these techniques to make money in all types of market environments. The goal of this book will be to help you have your money work for you.

Day trading sounds glamorous and exciting but the reality is that it is a grind. Even the top traders go through difficult stretches and dry spells similar to a batting slump in baseball. It makes you question your approach and abilities. I believe that is why there is a such a proliferation of day trading teachers and gurus out there. They realize how difficult it is to be consistent and therefore teach others to provide some steadiness to their income along the way. I am not saying these traders are lying about their trading success. I believe, in most cases, they are great traders who are very successful over time. My only point is that it can be a difficult road to be consistent in that arena. I prefer a style that uses similar techniques and strategies but in a way that still allows you to do other things during the day. The approach used by short term traders can be applied to long term investing by simply using longer time frames. For example, instead of looking at a 10 minute chart and a 2 minute chart of a stock, some investors could view a monthly chart and a weekly chart using the same techniques. In essence, seeing the market through multiple time frames will provide the trader the ability to time their investments like a professional. Improved timing will help your returns and stress levels whether you are holding an investment for a few days or for a year. This will be discussed in great detail in the following pages.

Please understand that professional traders take losses. They understand that losses are a necessary part of their business. However, these losses are comparatively small to the size of their gains. It is imperative to understand this point because any approach applied to the stock market will provide its share of losses over time. However, this is not reason enough to discard the method. The techniques in this book will allow an investor to have the confidence to invest in individual stocks or ETF's and make money consistently over time. These techniques can be used for swing trading (2-10 days) or long term investing (lasting months to years) and everything in between.

This methodology will not get you rich overnight. However, it is a sensible approach which will allow the average investor the ability to compound their money at a rate they would never have believed possible. It will also allow the professional institutional investor the ability to apply technical analysis to his already existing fundamental approach. Additionally, these techniques can be used with fundamental analysis without causing the fundamentalist to make significant changes to their existing investment style. Instead, it can be overlaid to improve the timing of the investments.

I have been using the techniques in this book during the past thirty years to help bank trust departments, mutual funds, hedge funds, and independent money managers with the timing of their fundamental buys and sells.

WHY TECHNICAL ANALYSIS IS NEEDED

For more than thirty years, I have had the pleasure of working with some of the best portfolio managers in the world. Many of them have been on the cover of Barron's, The Wall Street Journal or have been interviewed on CNBC. My conclusion is that, with a few exceptions, the best money managers use both fundamentals and technicals together. An investor who has confidence in identifying which stocks to buy and the patience to wait for the technicals to agree with their fundamental conclusions has a distinct advantage over the competition.

I have had many investors, both individual and institutional, tell me that they do not believe in technical analysis. While I am not going to say that using technical analysis is for everyone, I do believe that it will help in most cases. I have watched long term professional investors follow their fundamental models and evaluations without the help of technical analysis and it has hurt their timing and their performance in most cases.

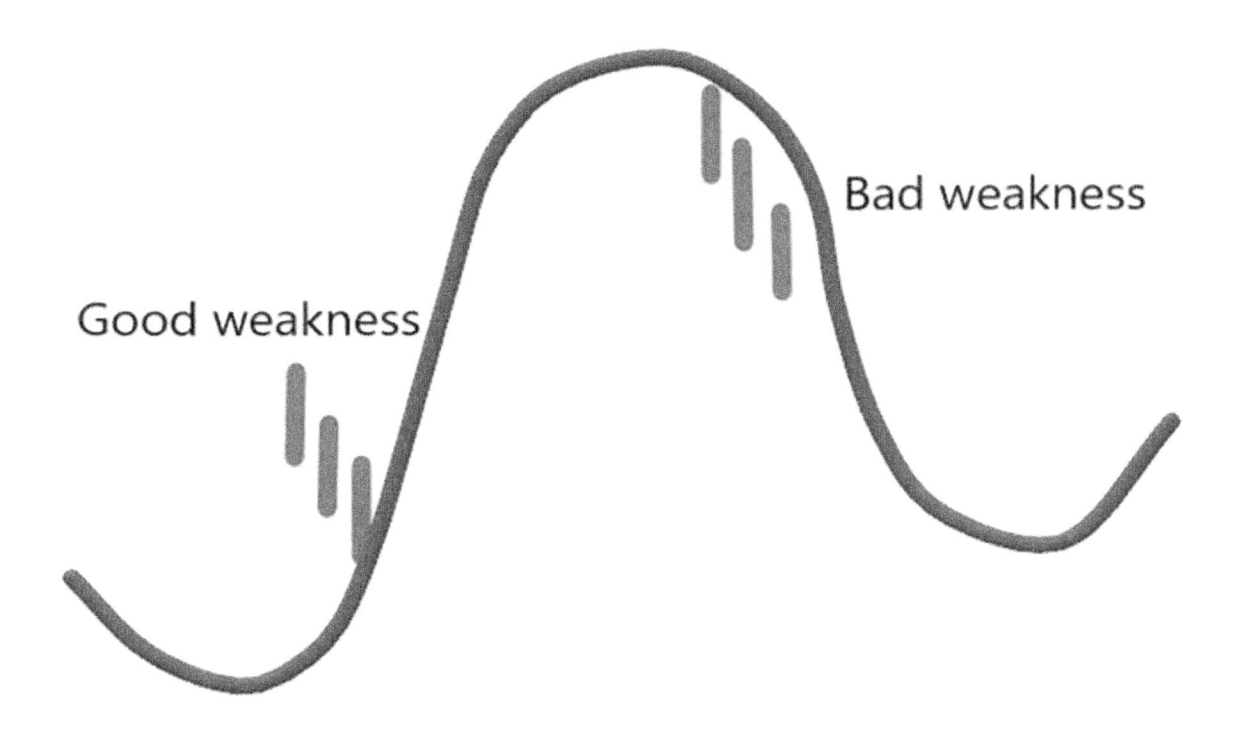

Understanding where a stock is positioned in relation to its long-term trend will help to identify whether a decline in the stock is a buying opportunity or not. The chart above shows the long-term trend (line). The bars are examples of a stock declining on this chart where the first would be considered good weakness - a buying chance - while the second is bad weakness - likely something that has more downside risk in the coming weeks or months. Keep in mind, for a shorter-term trader, the long-term trend is derived from a daily chart or an hourly chart as opposed to a monthly or weekly. The process of analysis is the same but the time frames change.

After working with some of the best fundamental investors in existence over the past three decades, I have found that their fundamental models can often be early since the stock will pass the screen as price is moving down to their fundamental buy level. The problem is that this drop sometimes coincides with a break of key support and when that occurs the decline can continue to weaken over the next three to six months.

Warren Buffett, one of the great investors of our time, has been successful without the use of technical analysis. However, the average investor must keep in mind that he has deep pockets. He will add to his losers until they turn around. Kraft Heinz Company (KHC) is shown below. This is one of his investments which he has owned for a long time. I am not trying to find flaws in Buffett's approach. In fact, his long-term performance speaks for itself. Nonetheless, it is important to realize that most investors cannot stomach a 50-75% drop in a stock and have the faith to see it through or keep buying. Most will give up at some point when the severity of the drop gets to be too much to stomach.

Incorporating technical analysis into your approach will help to eliminate this scenario. In fact, this method, when applied correctly should be reflected in small losses when compared to the size of your average gain. The most important factor is that it allows you to define the risk before you buy the stock. Being very diligent about the loss side of the equation and keeping them manageable is probably the most significant factor in your success over the long term.

Obviously, this book is not just for long term fundamental investors. It is also for the average investor who would like to improve their timing and entries for trades lasting a few days, weeks or months but may not have the time to sit in front of their screen all day and monitor their holdings.

Personally, I do not use fundamental analysis other than to know what industry a company is in and its market capitalization. Knowing the industry group and how other stocks in the group are trading is a helpful tool and has always been a part of my analysis since starting to incorporate technical analysis back in 1990. While this is clearly not in-depth analysis of the fundamentals, I am diligent about keeping my losses small and being very systematic about taking profits, which offers consistent returns over time.

The key is knowing yourself and your risk tolerance. If you are uncomfortable with being in a stock and having it pullback or correct against you for a few weeks or months, then you probably should be more focused on swing trading. If you are looking to place trades lasting a few days to a few weeks (Swing), you would use the trend of the daily chart to determine "Good weakness" or "Bad weakness" on a 60-minute chart. You need to be sure you know what you are trying to accomplish and have a written plan of action before putting any real money at risk.

One other important point is to realize that swing trading will have periods where it is very profitable and times where it is not. The marketplace shifts trends in both time and volatility. As a result, a factor in your success will be knowing where the trends exist and playing those trends. This means that you will be more successful and consistent by being willing to invest in different times frames, or if you are uncomfortable doing that, to stay in cash when the time frame you prefer is out of favor. I can tell you from experience that this is one of the most difficult things to learn. The need to have a trade/investment in place pulls you into buying when the overall conditions are not ideal and will hurt your chances of success. Patience to wait for the right conditions is one of the keys to successful investing.

A CHART IS A CHART

The goal of technical analysis, first, is to define the trend. I will show a few different methods for defining the trend in the coming pages. There are countless ways to define a trend but, in my view, keeping it as simple as possible should be the number one goal.

The second goal is to determine the strength of the trend. The strength of the trend is defined by its momentum. Later in this book, I will show a few different ways to determine the strength of a stock's trend. The momentum of a stock can be determined by comparing the most recent price legs, or by using momentum indicators such as MACD, ADX or RSI.

The final goal is to ascertain how long the trend has been in place. Knowing the length of the trend is vital because the longer a trend lasts, the higher the probability for a significant correction or a reversal to take place.

Below is a stock chart. I have erased the name, dates and time frames from the chart. This is just a set of open, high, low, close bars and a simple 18 moving average along with a simple 40 moving average. An

18 simple moving average (MA) takes the last 18 closing prices, adds them together and divides by 18. When plotted each day, we get a smoothed history of the closing prices over time. A simple 40 moving average (MA) is plotted the same way only using the past 40 closes in the calculation. Most investors that have read anything about moving averages are familiar with moving average crossover signals. Simply put, a crossover signal takes place when the 18 MA line crosses above or below the 40 MA line. These crossovers can be helpful in defining the trend of the stock. In addition, the slope of these MA lines, rising or falling, and the degree to which they are rising or falling also help with determining the strength of the trend. Regardless of whether these bars have developed over minutes or years, the pattern should be read the same way. Identifiable patterns take place whether these bars are hourly, daily, weekly, or monthly. The three arrows show where a crossover occurs AND the slope of the MA lines are in agreement with the crossover signal. This is where the trend is defined as positive or negative based on these parameters.

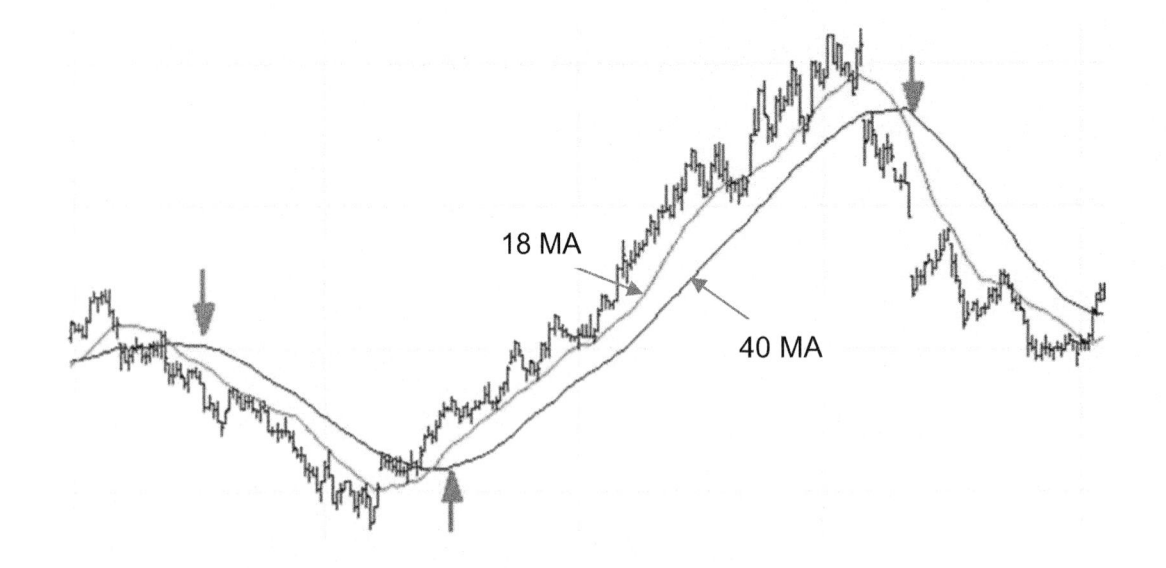

The slope of the moving averages (18 and 40 MA) and the price structure will change if I switch from a daily chart to a weekly chart, but the process of analysis is identical.

When evaluating a stock chart, the investor must know his or her own risk tolerance in order to determine what time frame is suitable. Generally, the longer the time frame, the larger the initial risk taken in each investment. However, the degree of accuracy typically improves. While minor swings may be manipulated at times, the long-term trend cannot be altered.

100 BARS ON A CHART

The following chart is a monthly chart of The Hershey Company (HSY). There are approximately 100 bars (monthly– open, high, low, and close) displayed in this time frame covering nearly 10 years. Price is well above the 18-month MA and 40-month MA. The 18-month MA is rising and above its 40-month MA, which shows the path of least resistance is to the upside. However, the price bars have been pulling back the past few months after a big upside run.

Monthly Time Frame

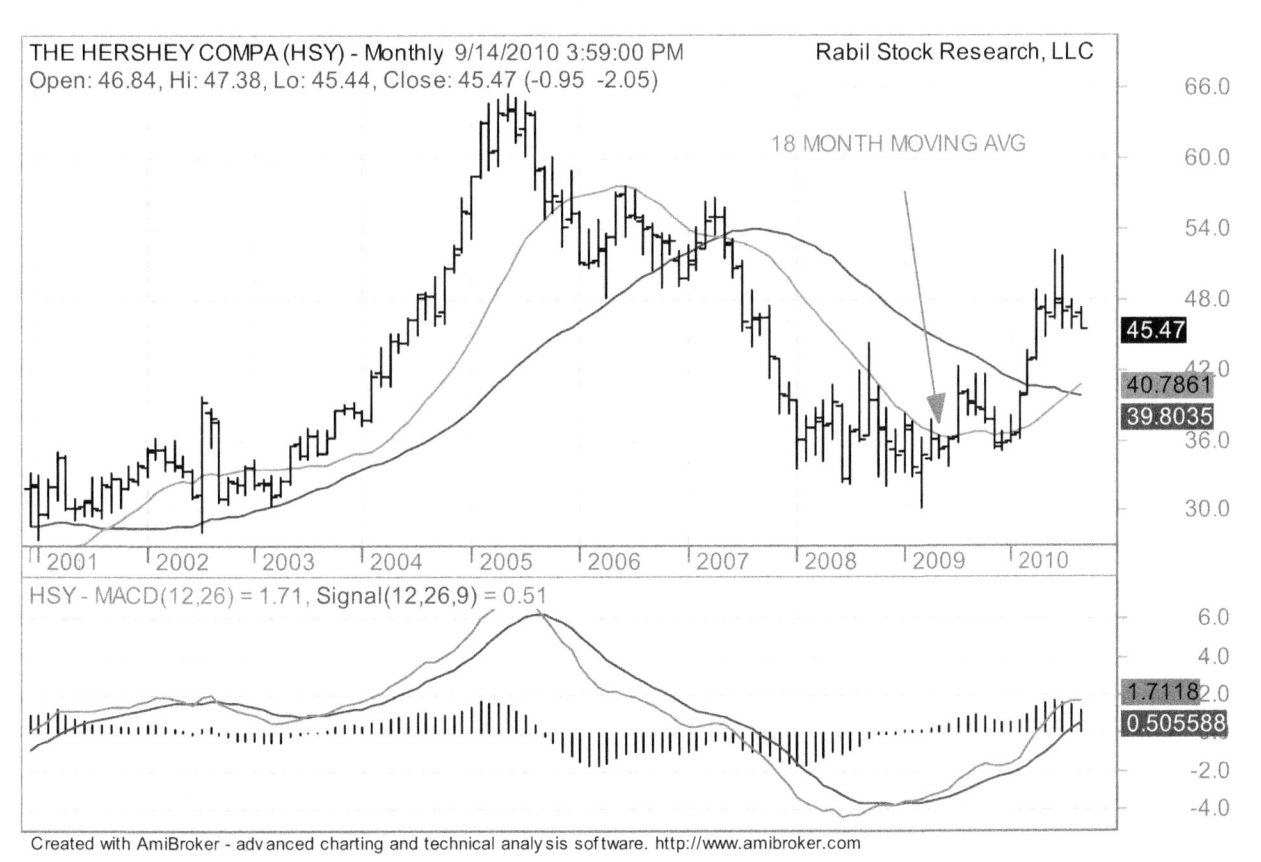

Weekly Time Frame

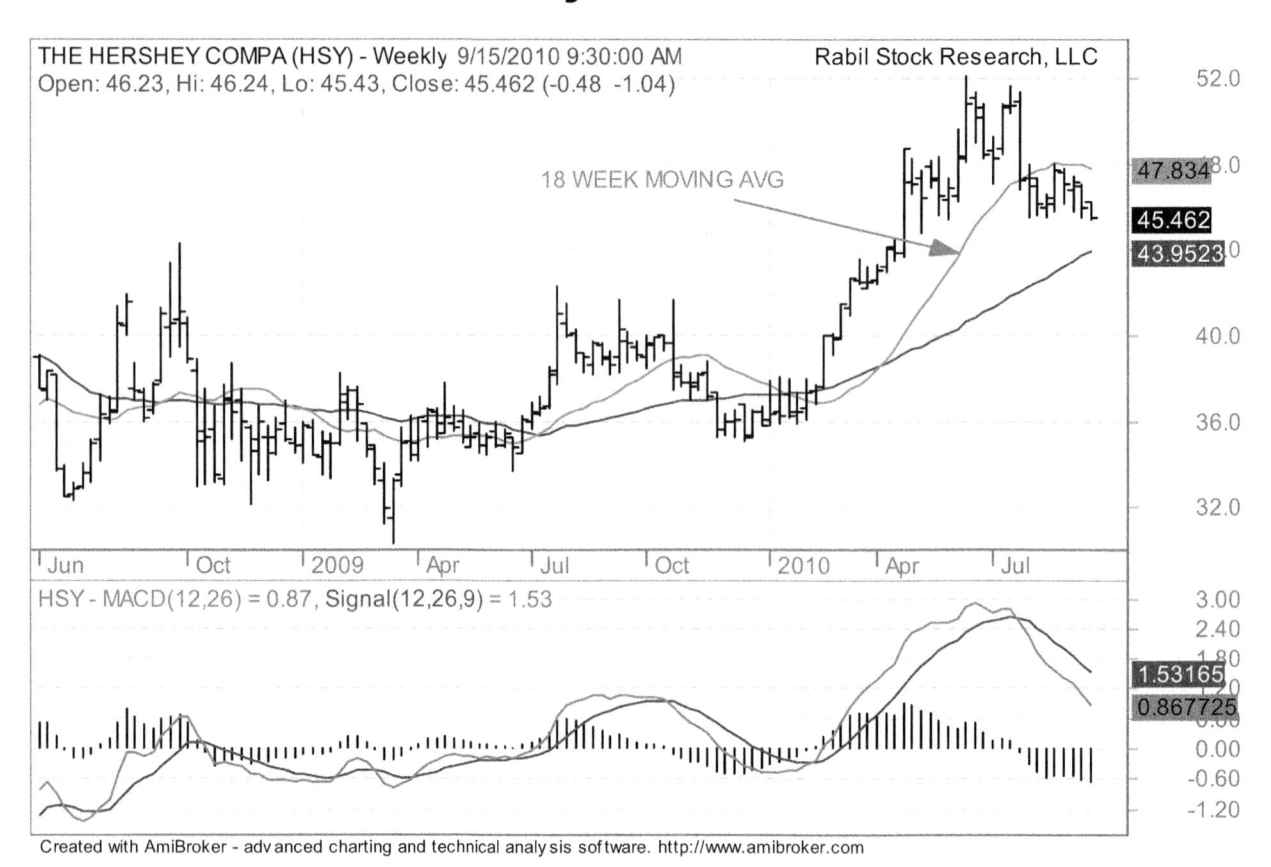

This is a weekly chart of HSY. There are approximately 100 bars (weekly– open, high, low, and close) displayed in this time frame covering a little over 2 years of time. The 18-week MA had been rising since early 2010 but has recently flattened out. So, in this time frame, the trend is neutral. The past 10 weeks have been spent in between the 18-week MA and a rising 40-week MA (blue). Price is clearly below the 18 MA in this time frame. At the same time, referencing the monthly chart on the previous page, price is above a rising 18-month MA. These are two different time frames providing two different price trends.

Daily Time Frame

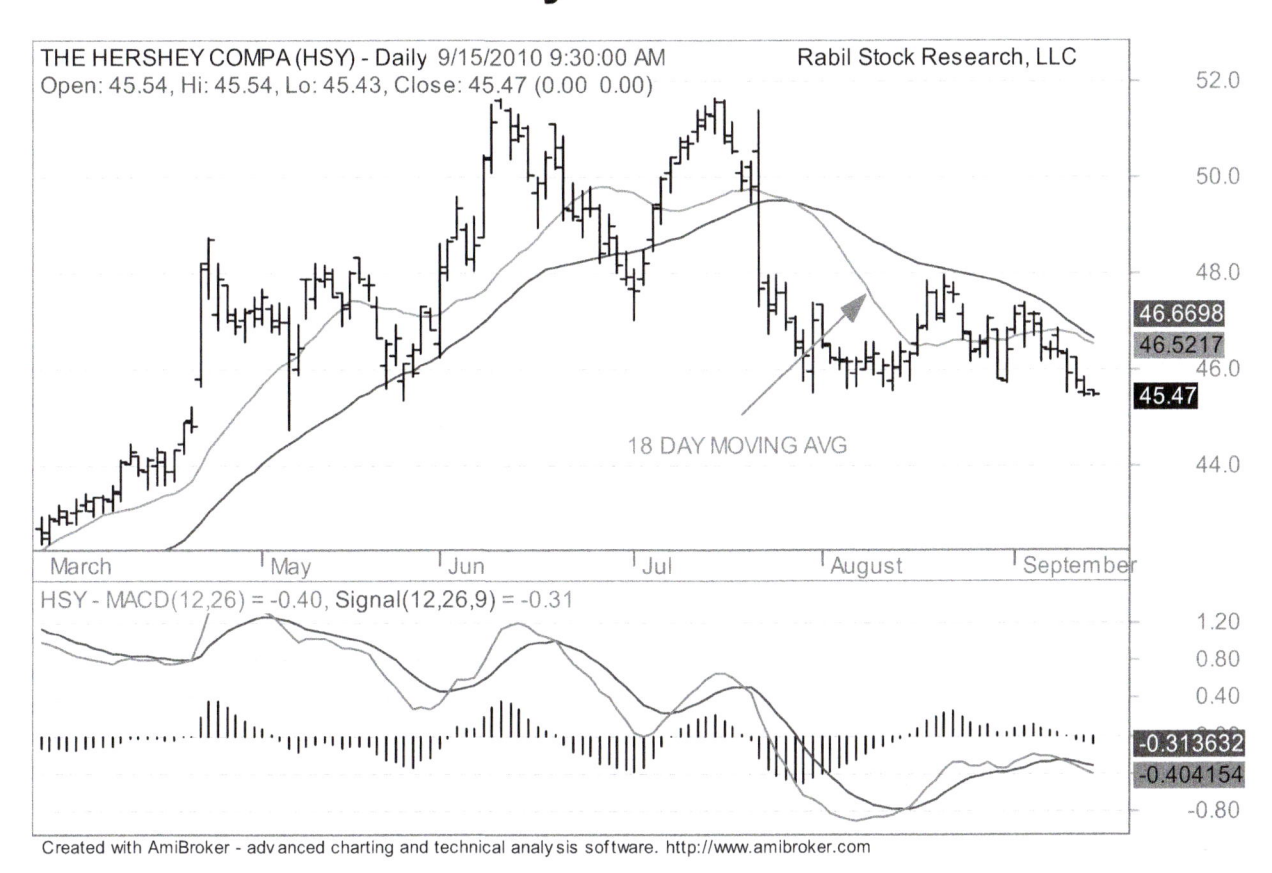

The last chart in this sequence is the daily of HSY. There are approximately 100 bars (daily– open, high, low, and close) displayed in this time frame covering approximately 6 months of information. In this time frame, the trend is down. Price is below the declining 18 and 40-day MA's and price continues to make lower highs and lower lows. A simple 2-3 bar pullback on a monthly chart turns the short-term trend negative in this case.

Understanding the different time frame's trends that are taking place at the same time is an advanced concept. There are plenty market professionals who have never seen TREND defined in these terms. My charting software allows me to have more than one chart displayed at a time. So, I have 4 charts together – monthly, weekly, daily, hourly. Each has the 18 and 40 MA on it. When displayed in this manner, multiple time frame confluence is much easier to recognize.

Confluence takes place when two consecutive time frames show trend indications that are in agreement. For instance, in the first quarter of 2010, Hershey's price was above a rising 18-month MA and above a rising 18-week MA line. This type of trend alignment helps to improve timing and accuracy. The explanation of multiple time frame analysis and how to implement it gets a little more complicated as we move through this book but the concept of aligning trends is fairly simple if you stay focused on the trend of each time frame individually before trying to combine them.

[TIME FRAME CONFLUENCE]

TREND

The goal of investing is to find low-risk, high reward entries. Granted, managing and exiting positions are extremely important skills as well. However, a good entry makes the process much easier. The first step in this process is to identify the trend of the stock or market you are thinking of buying. I have touched on the use of moving averages as a way of defining trend. However, there are many methods to achieve similar feedback.

I have been influenced by several great traders and teachers, including W.D. Gann, Victor Sperandeo, Linda Raschke, Dave Landry, Kevin Haggerty and Stan Weinstein. Each of these market professionals agrees that *PRICE* is the ultimate factor that determines if stock is in an uptrend, downtrend, or transition.

Google Inc (GOOG) – Daily

The chart of Google shows price only. It is clear based on this chart that GOOG is currently in an uptrend. The stock is moving from the lower left side of the page to the upper right and it is making higher price peaks and higher price valleys. It is best to keep technical analysis simple. I have been telling clients for years that PRICE and VOLUME studies are the foundation to good technical analysis. Before one starts to study indicators, I recommend first becoming an expert on price and volume.

In today's computerized world, many of the software programs can be programmed to identify price trends assuming one knows how to do it. As described earlier, moving averages work very well for this purpose. I have drawn trendlines on tens of thousands of charts over the years and I still do. However, the proper use of moving averages can save a lot of time in this regard and reduce much of the ambiguity.

Another way of seeing and defining the trend is with the use of swings or waves. W.D. Gann referred to these reversals as swings. In the 1970's, Art Merrill wrote a book about this concept and referred to the changes in direction as filtered waves. Many software programs call this indicator a Zigzag. [filtered wave]

Above, the chart of Apple Inc. shows a 4% filtered wave overlaid onto the price chart. A filtered wave means that all movement which is less than the filter is ignored. In this case, any pullback of less than 4% does not create a wave. Notice during 2009 this stock made higher bottoms based on a 4% filter. Using this filtered wave theory (Art Merrill, *Filtered Waves- Basic Theory*), one can quickly ascertain the direction as well as the longevity of the trend of a given market.

Here is the same time period as the previous chart. However, this chart of Apple Inc. (AAPL) has our 2 simple moving averages, the 18-day moving average and the 40-day moving average. Notice that in

February the 18-day MA crossed over the 40-day MA and remained above for the entire year. This reflects the same positive feedback that we just discussed with a 4% filtered wave. These are two very different approaches to defining a trend, but both are very simple and the resulting signals are virtually identical in this case.

Why an 18 and a 40 MA? Why not a 20 and a 50 MA? Or exponential moving average? What about the 200-day MA? (one of the most widely used MA lines). These are valid questions. Using a 20 and 50 instead of 18 and 40 would work fine. Frankly the difference between an 18 MA and a 20 MA is quite negligible. Put both on a chart at the same time and you will see what I mean. I favor the 18 MA simply because the slope shift is a little quicker than the popular 20 MA. In addition, for this method of using 2 moving averages together like a buddy system, I have found the simple MA lines to be more useful then the Exponential version. Again, it is a personal thing and the use of EMA's (lines which give more weight to the most recent closes in a sequence rather than weighting them all equally like the simple average) can be employed with success but you will probably need to adjust the length to make the signals a little more comparable.

In my opinion, moving averages should not be used as an exact science. In fact, technical analysis in general, while having various quantitative benefits, is probably best when not used as an exact science either. The question of the 200-day MA is easy to answer. If we display a weekly chart with 18 and 40 MA's, the 200-day MA is shown in the form of the 40-week MA. I prefer to use multiple time frames in my analysis because it has proven to be very helpful in refining my stock selection and timing process. Having the ability to look at each individual time frame and its own structure, price action and momentum is useful information when trying to find key inflection points. This will become clearer as I give more examples throughout the text. Also, I will show why I use the 40 MA together with the 18 MA later in the book.

The Key to Trend Analysis

As I mentioned earlier, the difference between the 18 moving average and the 20 moving average is very small. I believe the techniques described in this book can be employed by any intermediate term moving average line – 18 to 22 periods in length. If you prefer to use a 20 MA instead of 18 MA, that is fine. However, stick with it. Please do not switch back and forth. Your mind will learn to assimilate to whichever MA lines you choose. But, if you continue to switch the lines, your subconscious mind will never be of service. I know from my own experience after using the same MA lines in viewing millions of charts over the years that there are times where I know what is coming (an intuitive feeling) but I have a difficult time explaining it to my clients in the form of hard facts. This is the subconscious mind taking over and it can be a powerful tool in chart reading. It will only work after your mind has processed thousands and thousands of charts which have the same look to them.

Whichever length you choose, this intermediate term moving average is the most important component in this strategy. While I use the 18 MA and the 40 MA as a buddy system, it is the 18 MA which really drives this approach. The position of the 18 MA on the monthly chart will play a large role in defining your longer-term investment strategy for a given instrument. It has the same effect as the wind blowing at your back when riding a bike. If you have ever tried to ride a bike on open road with the wind in your face, this will give you the sensation of what it is like to make a long-term investment when the 18-month MA is working against you, i.e. bad weakness. There are very few exceptions to this rule.

The monthly chart of Amazon (AMZN) below shows what can take place when the 18-month MA line is working for you. This line has been rising since 2009 except for a pause in 2014 where it flattened but never turned down. As long as this MA has good upward slope, the long-term trend is bullish with good momentum. The slope of this line is important to monitor. I have bolded the line on the next few charts to show that the 18 MA on each timeframe is the driver for this approach and quite often will be the same as the trendline if it were drawn in. Also, it tends to

provide support on pullbacks when it is rising and offers resistance on rallies when it is declining. It is a moving line so it is an area of support/resistance as opposed to an exact level.

The monthly chart of Walmart (WMT) is a good example of how the slope of the 18 MA helps to provide a bias for the long-term trend. Since we are using an 18-month MA, it is considered the long-term trend. An 18-week MA would be considered the intermediate-term trend. The first shading on the WMT chart shows a flat period for this MA line and that puts the bigger picture trend in the neutral camp until the breakout in early 2012. Then, in late 2014, a sharp selloff turned the 18-month MA lower. There was no

confirming price evidence of a change in trend (explained in the next section). The decline reversed back to the upside after spending significant time shifting the slope of the 18-month MA line back up in early 2017 (second shaded area). The act of turning this monthly line is time consuming and often provides plenty of time to monitor while this process takes place. In this example, it took nearly a year to turn from the point that rallied up to it for the first time in 2016. Note that when this line turned higher, it became nice support on two deep pullbacks during 2018.

DEFINITIONS FOR A CHANGE IN TREND

The following is a description of what is required in order to define a trend, as well as a depiction of the steps necessary in order to change an existing trend. A clear understanding of the following charts will provide the investor with a solid foundation of how to make money over the long term. Understanding price structure is the single most important piece of knowledge an investor can have to improve his ability to be profitable over time. I have found that many investors want to jump ahead and learn about all types of indicators before they truly understand the basics. If you can learn the 'Fundamentals of Technicals' you will do much better than someone who only has a cursory knowledge of numerous types of indicators.

In 2013, when Peyton Manning, the quarterback for the Denver Broncos, was asked how he was able to come back from four neck surgeries and play at as high a level as he did prior, he said he remained focused on the basics. He said upon his return from neck surgery, he spent countless hours working on his fundamentals with his college quarterback coach.

This is the approach I recommend for really learning technical analysis. Making money in the stock market is about having confidence in your approach through 'thick and thin' and that starts with a deep understanding of the basics. These graphs are going to look too basic to have any real meaning. Please do not be fooled by the simplicity.

The concepts below are adapted from Vic Sperandeo, "Trader Vic – Methods of a Wall Street Master", another outstanding book.

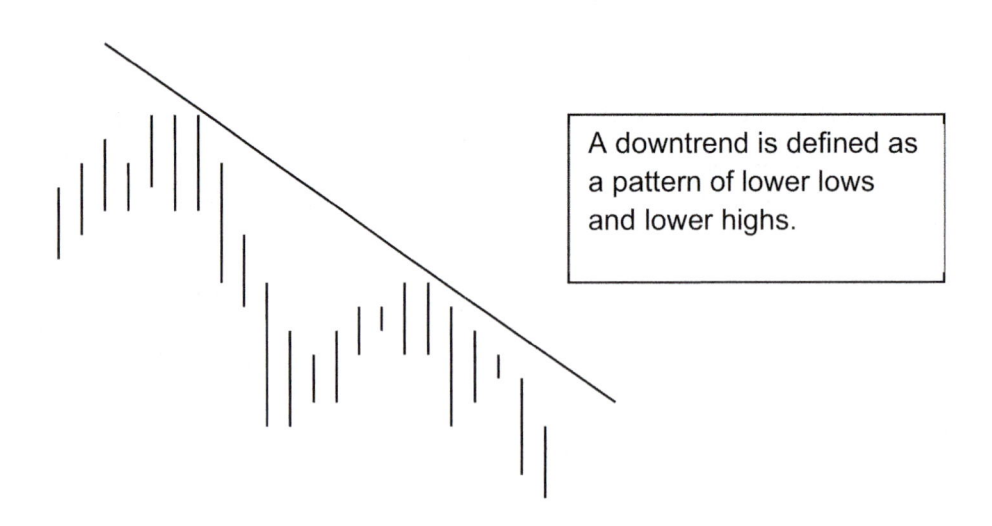

A downtrend is defined as a pattern of lower lows and lower highs.

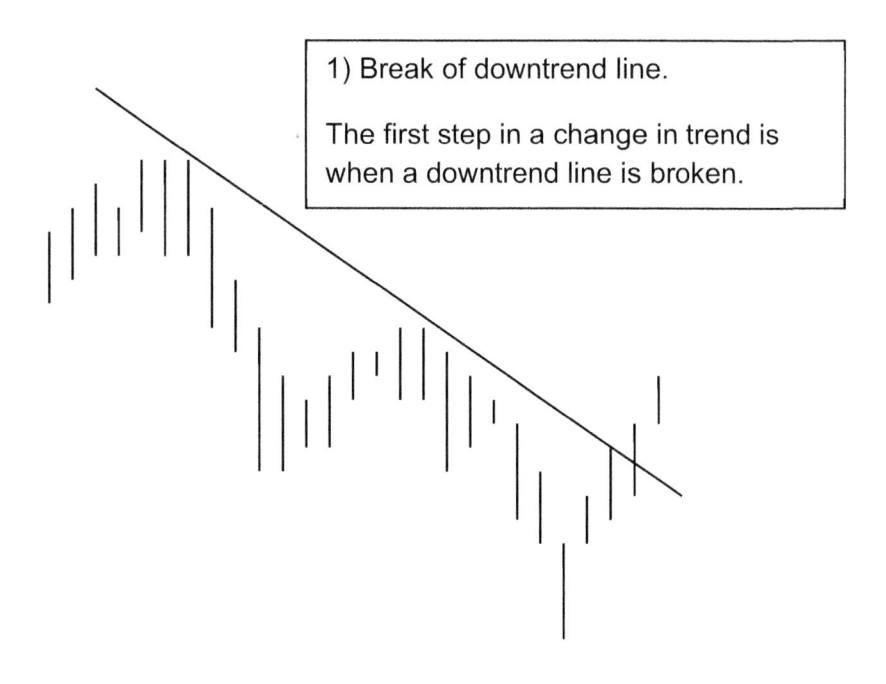

1) Break of downtrend line.

The first step in a change in trend is when a downtrend line is broken.

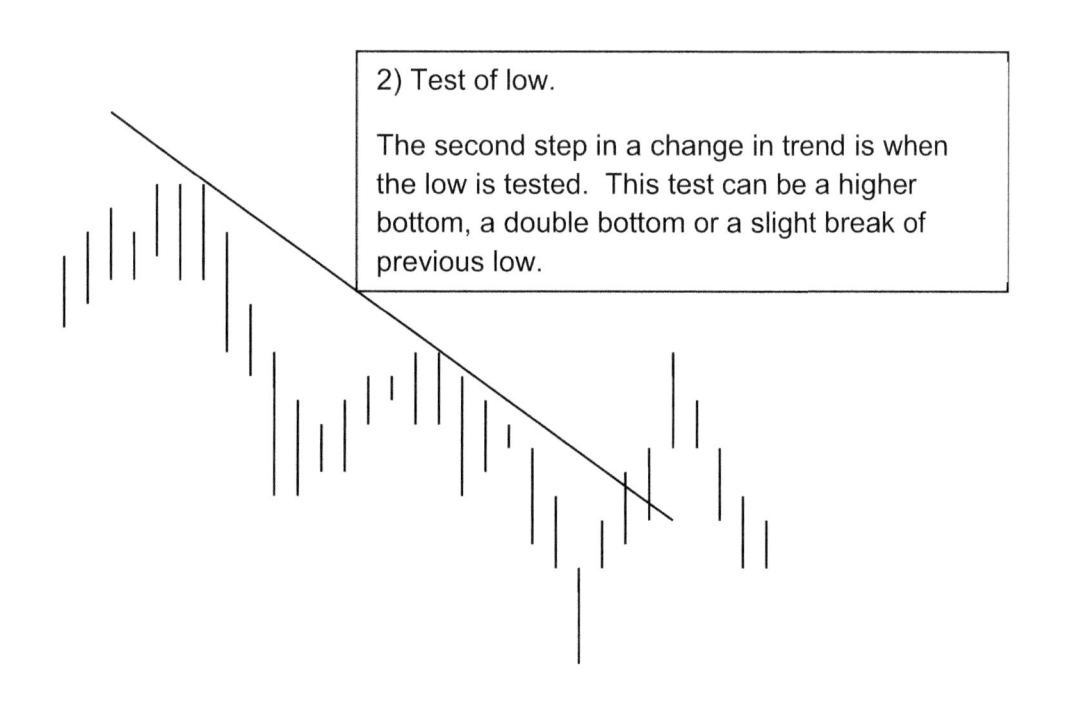

2) Test of low.

The second step in a change in trend is when the low is tested. This test can be a higher bottom, a double bottom or a slight break of previous low.

3) Break above Previous Top.

The third and confirming step in a change in trend takes place when a higher high is made above the previous top.

As you can clearly see, we now have an uptrend in place. The same rules now apply in reverse in order to see a bearish change in trend develop.

This method of trend change is only presumptive evidence of a change in trend since we need a series of higher highs and higher lows to have a confirmed trend. A series would be a minimum of two. However, when using multiple time frames, the method described in the charts above becomes important for providing trigger mechanisms to enter in the direction of the higher time frame trend with lower risk. This will make more sense as we move through numerous examples in this manual. The concepts above are extremely important to understand. I recommend studying and practicing the ability to identify these reversals on daily and weekly charts of stocks that you have an interest. You will want to build up the skill of seeing the change in trend develop without the use of anything else but price. Then, when MA lines are drawn, the overall price structure and trend will make much more sense to you.

The following daily chart of Johnson & Johnson (JNJ) depicts the change of trend pattern taking place in real life. These patterns develop on all times every day. I have overlaid a filtered wave so the shift and key points are simpler to recognize. As you study more examples, the 1-2-3 pattern will become easier and easier to identify. 1 signifies the break of the downtrend line. 2 is considered the test. 3 is the higher high which significantly increases the odds that a change in trend has taken place, and 4 is the confirming evidence with a second higher high and higher low following the trendline break.

It is important to understand that each of these levels can be used for entry. Entering at 1 would be the earliest and riskiest trigger point. As each part of the sequence unfolds, there are new entry points and the odds increase as we move forward. As you can see, you pay for confirmation. In other words, by waiting for confirmation, you will typically pay higher prices but you will have a higher probability of being right. We will be using this trend change analysis as a trigger on the weekly time frame when the monthly chart is telling us that the trend is turning or is in a bullish trend (or on a daily chart when the weekly is turning or bullish). As a result, it is not necessary to wait for full confirmation on the lower time frame. I tend to favor entering after 2 is confirmed by turning up and making a new bottom. This often provides the best reward-to-risk scenario when combining two consecutive time frames. This will be discussed in more detail later.

Home Depot (HD) is shown above and the change in trend pattern develops in early 2019. Notice the difference in entry price buying at 2 vs 4. As I mentioned early, you have to pay for confirmation.

The weekly chart of Procter & Gamble (PG) is shown below. There are three change in trend sequences which take place over the course of five years on this chart. An important point to note is the second step in changing a trend (2), which is the test, oftentimes may only be 1/3 of a retracement of the prior move. It can be quick and sometimes difficult to recognize using price alone.

Later, I will show how moving averages can offer an advantage at recogzing this test a little more easily in certain cases.

Study the above charts in this section several times before moving on. As mentioned earlier, I would recommend pulling up charts of several stocks and seeing if you can identify this 1-2-3 change in trend pattern taking place on any of them. I would also advise using daily, weekly and monthly time frames for this exercise. You will see that daily trends can be much more volatile and erratic. Weekly trends are much more reliable than daily trends. While monthly trends provide very dependable trends, they often take a long time to shift. As a result, I look at the monthly chart for clues that a change may be coming and then use the signals on the weekly chart to work the two-time frames in concert with one another.

In addition, do not get obsessed with drawing the perfect trendline. Just connect the last two most obvious rising bottoms in an uptrend and connect the two most obvious declining tops in a downtrend. If you cannot find declining tops or rising bottoms, this likely means the trend is neutral or sideways. [In this case, you want to try to determine the upper and lower boundaries of this range and draw these horizontal trendlines in place.] For instance, if steps 1 and 2 have been completed for a change in trend but not step 3, then this chart is in transition until the upper or lower boundary is clearly broken as in the example of SWM below.

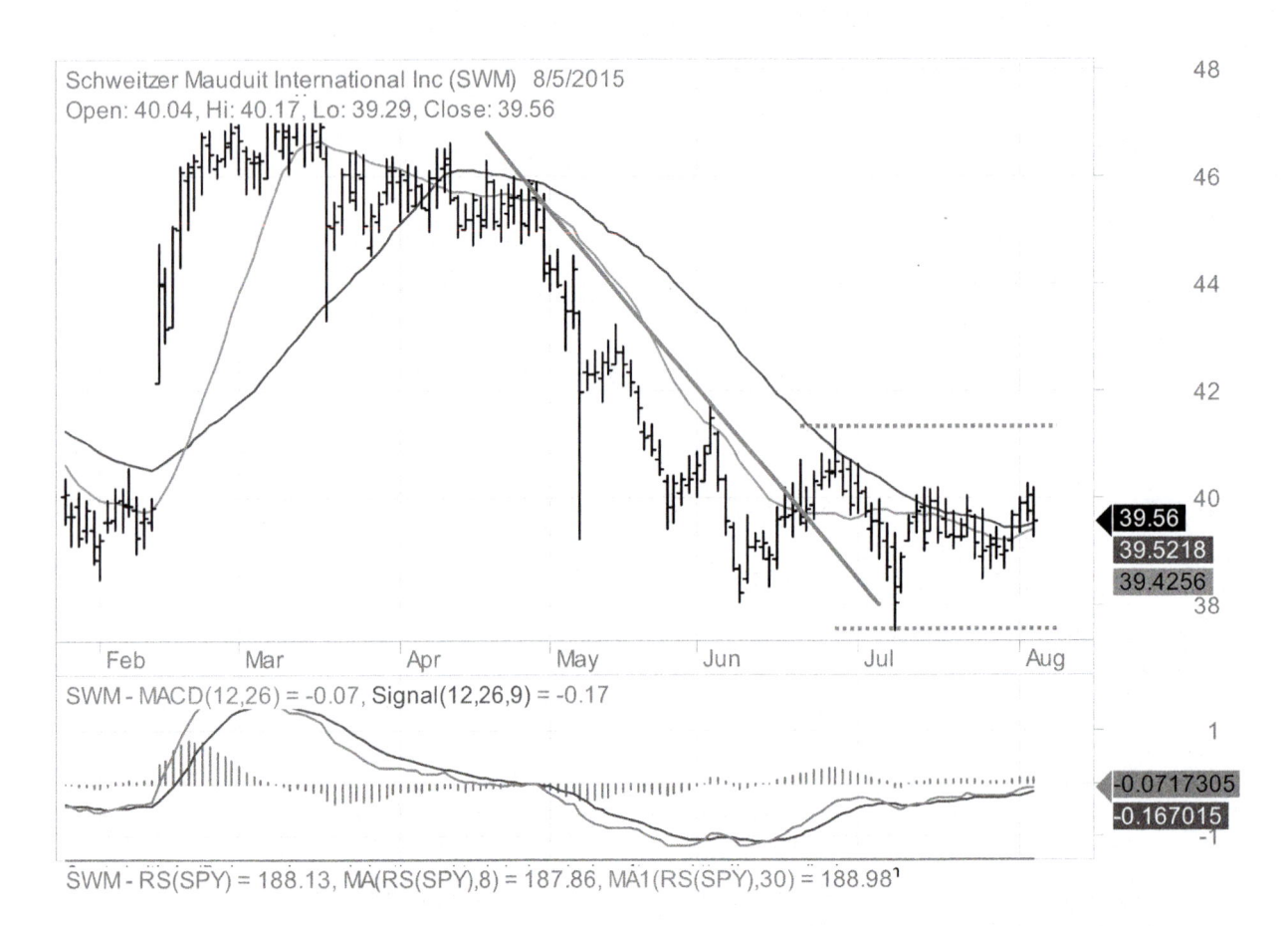

Schweitzer Mauduit International (SWM) – Daily

RULES FOR MULTIPLE TIME FRAMES

Rule 1 - Every time frame has its own structure as well as support and resistance levels.

A simple way to see price structure is by using the filtered wave theory described earlier. The waves for each time frame will be different since each wave is trying to closely mimic the key turning points for the specific time frame. The turning points for these waves are considered important support/resistance levels since they were strong enough to cause a reversal.

The above chart is the daily of The Hershey Company (HSY) with the wave structure and support and resistance lines. The line connects the highs and lows of each wave in the price structure which helps to define the trend. This shows the price peaked in Feb 2014 at $108.69 and made a lower high followed by a lower low bottoming at $87.88 at the end of July 2014. Since that time the price waves have made a higher low and a higher high. The reversal point for each wave is considered support/resistance on that time frame. As you can see, in this time frame, there are several horizontal lines drawn depicting potential support and resistance levels.

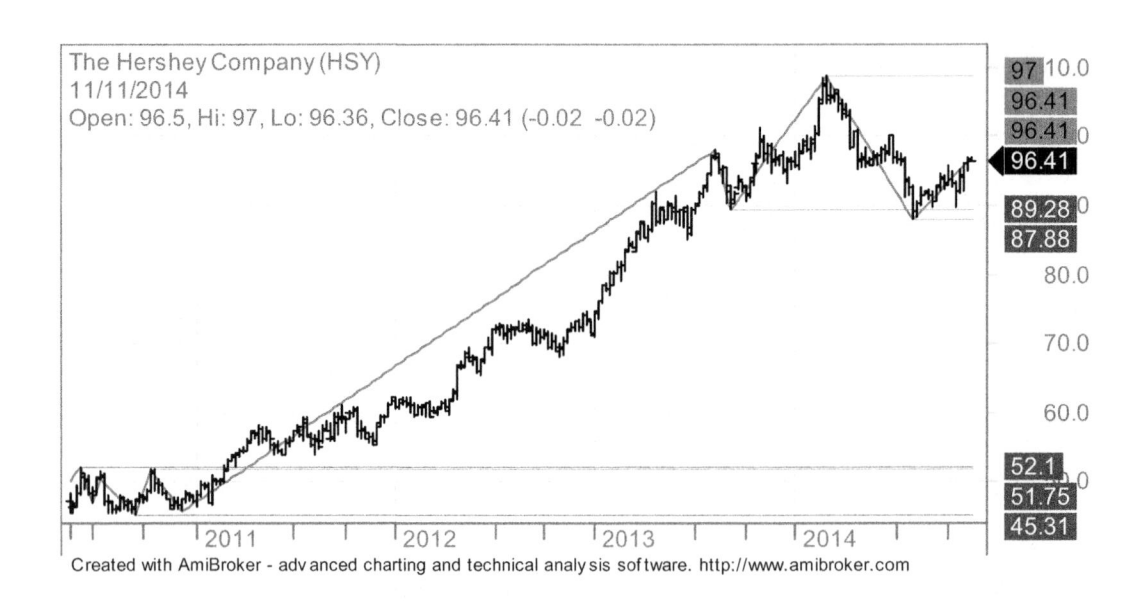

This chart is the weekly of The Hershey Company (HSY) with its wave structure and support/resistance lines. Notice how much less noise there is on the weekly time frame during 2014. The daily chart had several waves during 2014 but the weekly only had one top and one bottom. As a result, we can see that the price structure is unique to each time frame and key support and resistance lines are different as well. It is important to recognize that key turning points will display differently in each time frame. In this case, the weekly chart shows the two most important reversal levels of 2014. This should be factored into any decision when looking the daily chart. We always want to look up a time frame to see key levels of support and resistance. In addition, we want to identify the trend based on the wave structure of the higher time frame. In general, it is best to trade when both time frames are shifting their trend simultaneously, but this happens less frequently. Instead, we can use key support and resistance lines on the higher time frame to help decide whether the trade has the proper risk/reward characteristics on the lower time.

Rule 2 - The higher time frames overrule the lower time frames.

Rule 2 means that if we have a buy signal on the daily chart and a sell signal on the weekly chart at the same time, the weekly chart wins. Exxon Mobil Corp. (XOM) below has a bullish crossover on the daily chart at the same time there is a bearish crossover on the weekly chart. We do not want to buy this daily signal when it is essentially giving the same signal in the opposite direction on the weekly chart.

Exxon Mobil Corp. (XOM) – *daily chart with 18 MA crossing above the 40 MA line.*

Exxon Mobil Corp. (XOM) – *weekly chart with 18 MA crossing down below the 40 MA line.*

In fact, I will show you the tactics to take advantage of this scenario later in this manual. For now, just understand that <u>we never take a setup on a lower time frame (daily) if the higher time frame (weekly) is giving an opposing signal at the same time.</u>

Rule 3 - The trend and momentum of the higher time frame determines the direction and therefore the action taken on the lower time frame.

Using Apple Inc. (AAPL) from 1990-1991, this daily chart shows three arrows. The first points to where the trend on this time frame turns bearish. In this case, we would be looking at the hourly chart (lower time frame) for shorting opportunities while bearish conditions exist on the daily chart. Then, in the 4th quarter of 1990, the up arrow reflects the change in trend using the crossover and slope of the 18 MA and the 40 MA lines.

[handwritten: Trend line as a TI]

During this time, using Rule 3, we would only take buy signals on the hourly chart.

I would like to point out that the slope of these two MA lines were rising at about the same rate, almost parallel, with a comfortable distance between them. These are the characteristics of a strong trend. I will discuss momentum indicators later in the book that will help with this determination. However, having the ability to recognize a strong trend and its momentum using only price and MA lines is a clear advantage when you are trying to decide which higher time frame trends to play.

Our odds increase when the higher time frame trend (daily, in this case) and the trigger time frame (hourly) are in agreement. Finally, the last arrow signals the daily trend reversing to the downside again. At this point, we would be down on the hourly chart looking for high probability sell signals.

The higher time frame tells us there is a trend with good momentum and the pullbacks along the way provide an opportunity to find an entry on the trigger time frame. Your odds of finding winning trades, whether long term or short term, will increase significantly by using this rule. There will be many examples throughout the remainder of this manual of how to put this rule into practice.

INCORPORATING MOVING AVERAGES

Scot Lowry studied moving averages and their application to commodities. He wrote a book called "The Magic of Moving Averages." This is an outstanding book and helped give me a better understanding of how to use multiple times in my analysis. I have applied a few of the signals to stocks. While I have made a few modifications, the substance of his teachings is what follows in this section.

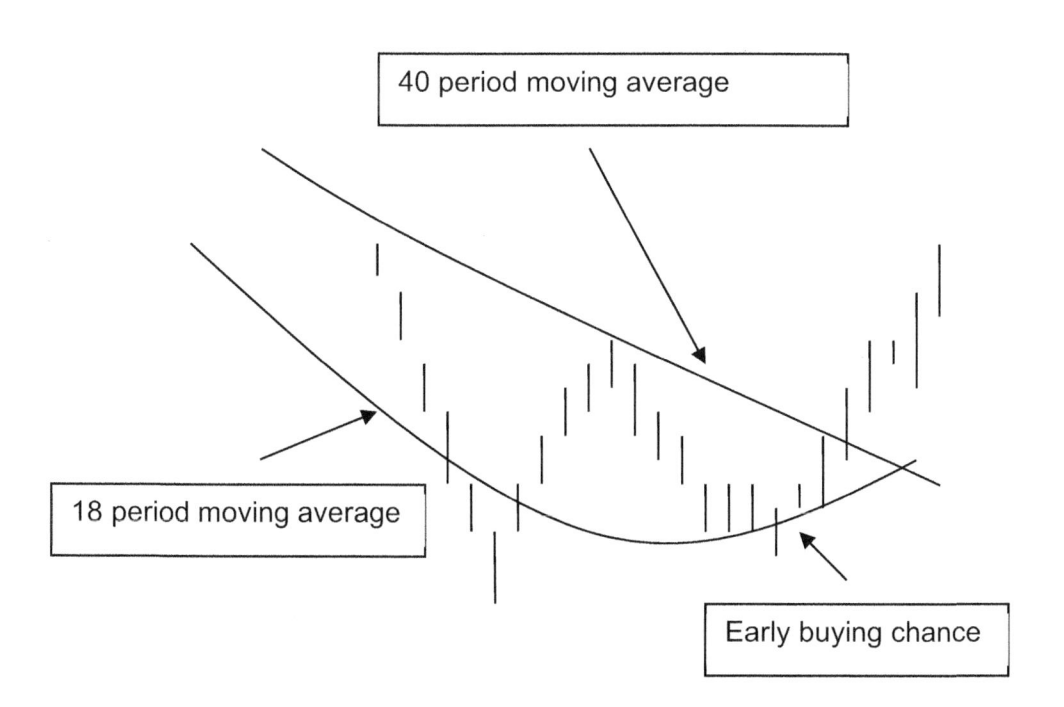

[Figure: Chart showing a 40 period moving average and 18 period moving average forming a curve over price bars, with an arrow indicating an "Early buying chance" where price meets the declining 40 period moving average after bouncing off the 18 period moving average.]

Lowry referred to this pattern as the '40 to 18 bounce.' Look for this setup following a big decline. Once a large decline has taken place, wait for the stock to rally all the way up to the 40-period moving average. After this rally has taken place, wait for a pullback to the 18-period moving average as a buy. What I have noticed is that when a stock rallies up to the 40 MA after a strong selloff, this rally often coincides with Step 1 in a change in trend - the break of the downtrend (see the weekly chart of INTC below).

As a result, looking to buy when the stock pulls back to the 18 MA will often coincide with the test of the low or Step 2 in a change in trend. I often use this signal on the longer-term time frame as an early sign that the trend is changing. It is important that the 18 MA is rising when price pulls back and I want this line to halt the pullback. When this condition exists on the higher time frame, I often see one of the next few patterns develop on the lower time frame and this confirms the buy. This can be the best opportunity to buy early in a new long-term uptrend since odds are improving that the trend is changing. (Apply this same approach to the negative side following a large up move in a stock or market).

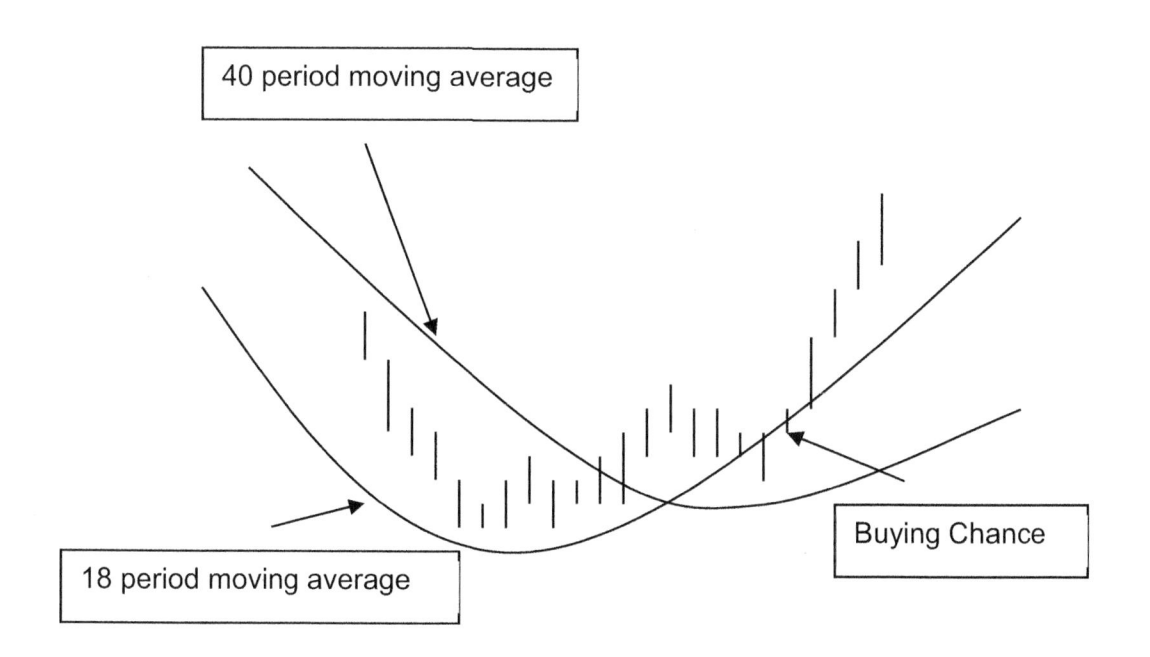

[Chart showing 40 period moving average, 18 period moving average, and Buying Chance]

The chart above shows a classic buying opportunity. This occurs when the 18-period moving average crosses above the 40-period moving average and the price then pulls back between the two and then emerges again. This pattern works best when the price enters 'the zone' between the 18 and 40 fairly quickly following the moving average crossover.

The daily chart of Intel Corp. (INTC) provides two nice examples of this operative buy signal.

It is imperative to use the next higher time frame to determine the trend and avoid taking signals against it (multiple time frames – Rule 3).

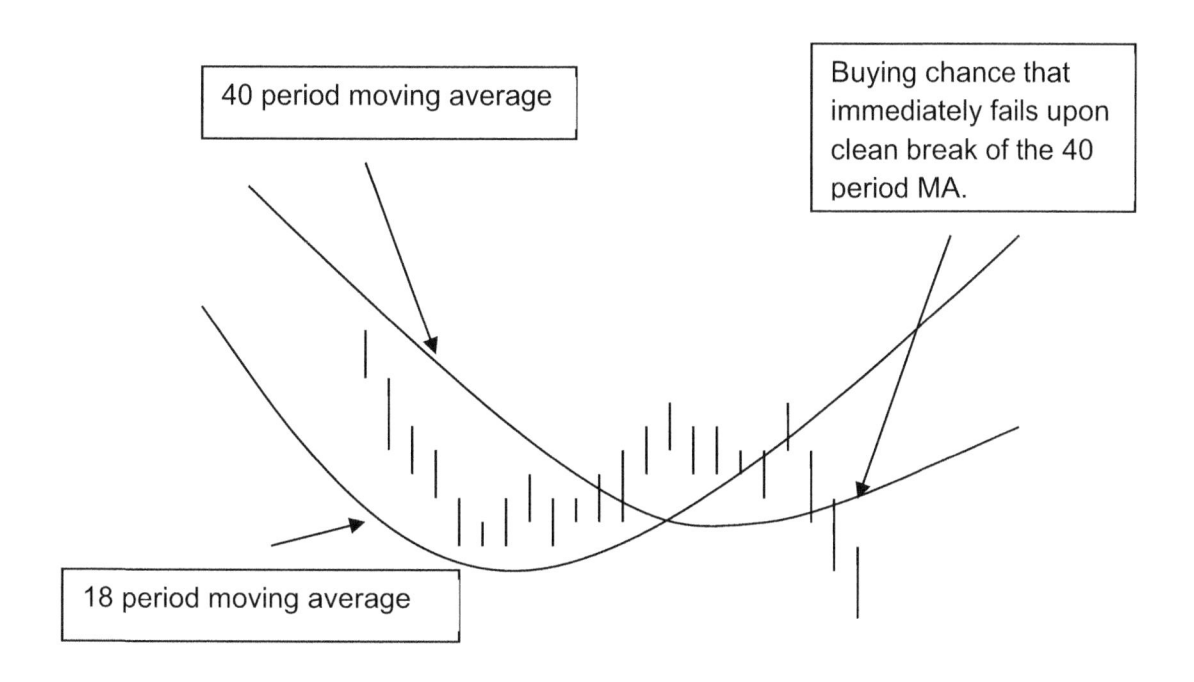

[40 period moving average]

[Buying chance that immediately fails upon clean break of the 40 period MA.]

[18 period moving average]

This pattern follows the previous one because it is a classic buy signal that fails. In this example, you must assume that the chart on the higher time frame is negative. If this is the case, you would ignore the bullish signal and instead be waiting for the bullish pattern to breakdown. A clean break of the 40-period moving average signals that the bullish signal has failed, and the trend is most likely resuming to the downside.

The daily chart of Exxon Mobil Corp. (XOM) gives a great example of this failed buy signal. First, notice the thick Moving Average line (arrow). This represents the trend on the weekly chart. The downward slope of this weekly MA means that we are only looking to take short trades on the daily chart. As a result, the classic buy signal would be ignored since it is going counter to the weekly trend. Instead, we would wait to see if the buy signal fails and look to enter short when price breaks down through the 40-day MA line.

The best buying opportunities for long term investors take place when a stock or ETF pulls back to a rising 18-month MA. This provides the long-term investor the opportunity to get aboard an already existing bullish trend with the lowest

risk. This is the time to be on the alert on the Weekly chart for bullish signals. The best selling opportunities (in the case of a short sale) take place when an issue rallies to a declining 18-month MA.

There is another situation where the 18-month MA is turning for the first time in at least a few years which can provide an outstanding early buying chance in a new trend. However, there are some other momentum signs that need to be in place to confirm this pattern. As previously discussed, if you prefer short time horizons, then simply drop down to the favored time frame.

The following pages give more graphic detail into how the moving averages should look in both time frames, higher and lower. The examples use the monthly and weekly time frame. However, it is important to reiterate that these patterns are the same in all time frames, even on an intraday level. Personally, I would not go below 5 minutes. The micro time frames are very noisy and subject to more false signals.

WEEKLY TREND IN RED

MONTHLY TREND IN BLUE

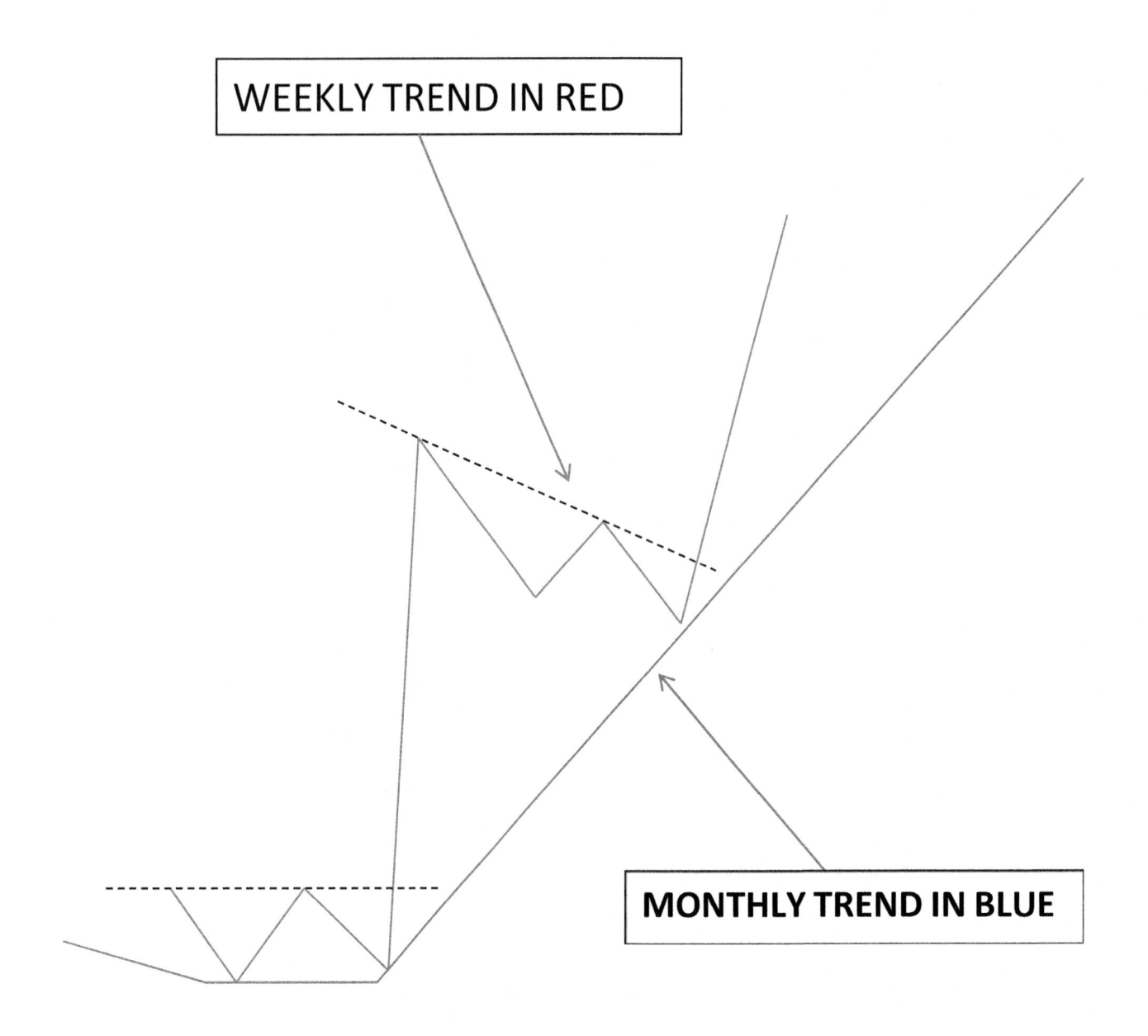

LOOK TO BUY CORRECTIONS IN THE WEEKLY TREND WHEN THE MONTHLY TREND IS BULLISH OR STARTING TO TURN BULLISH.

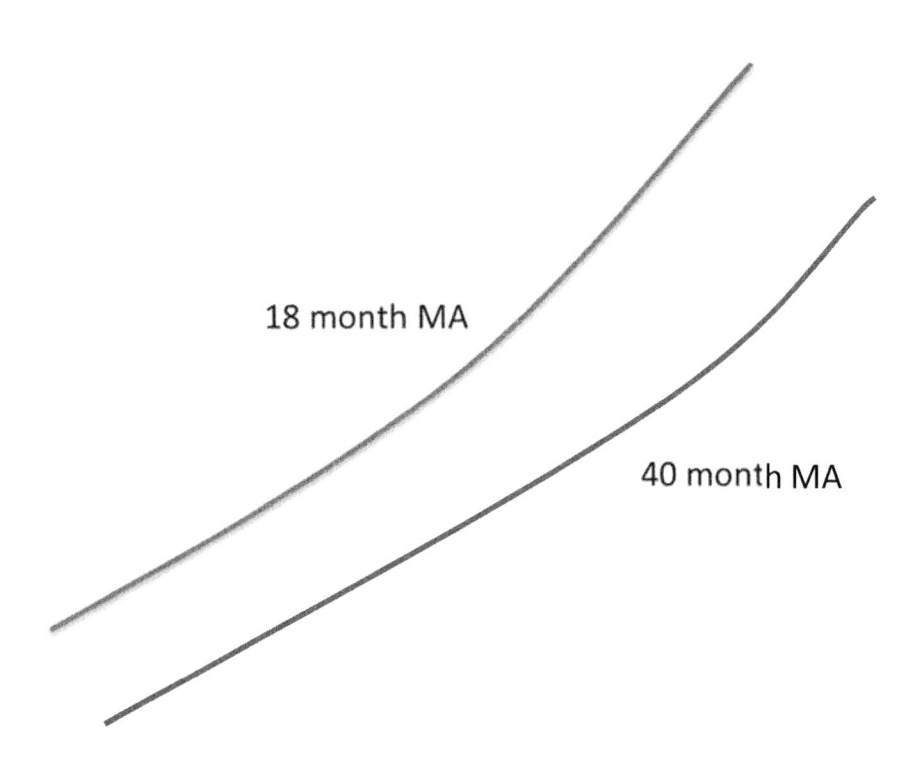

18 month MA

40 month MA

ABOVE THE 2 LINES SHOW WHEN THE MONTHLY IS TRENDING TO THE UPSIDE

BELOW THE 2 LINES SHOW WHEN THE MONTHLY TREND IS STARTING TO TURN

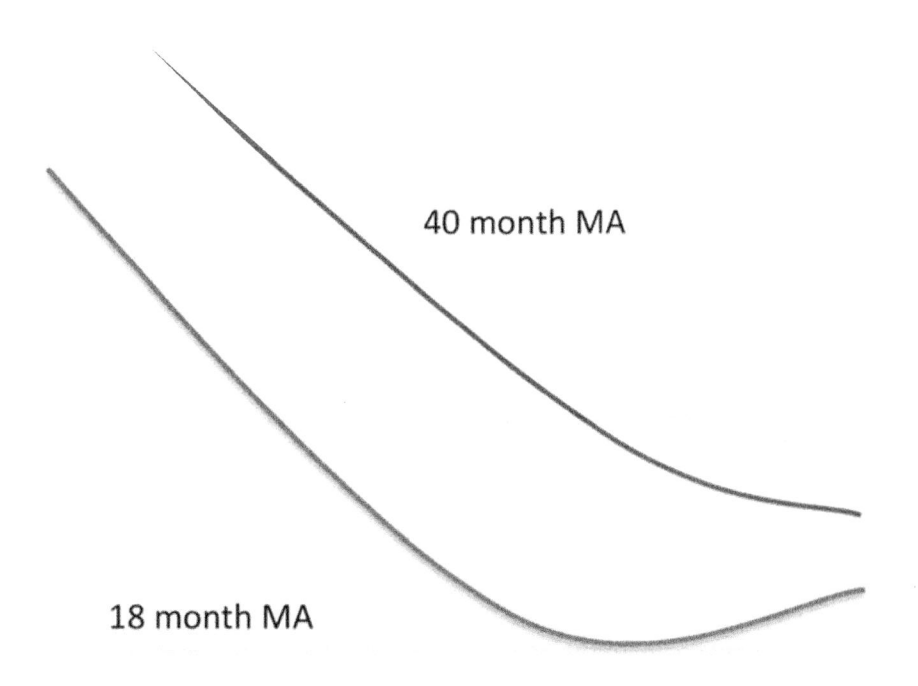

40 month MA

18 month MA

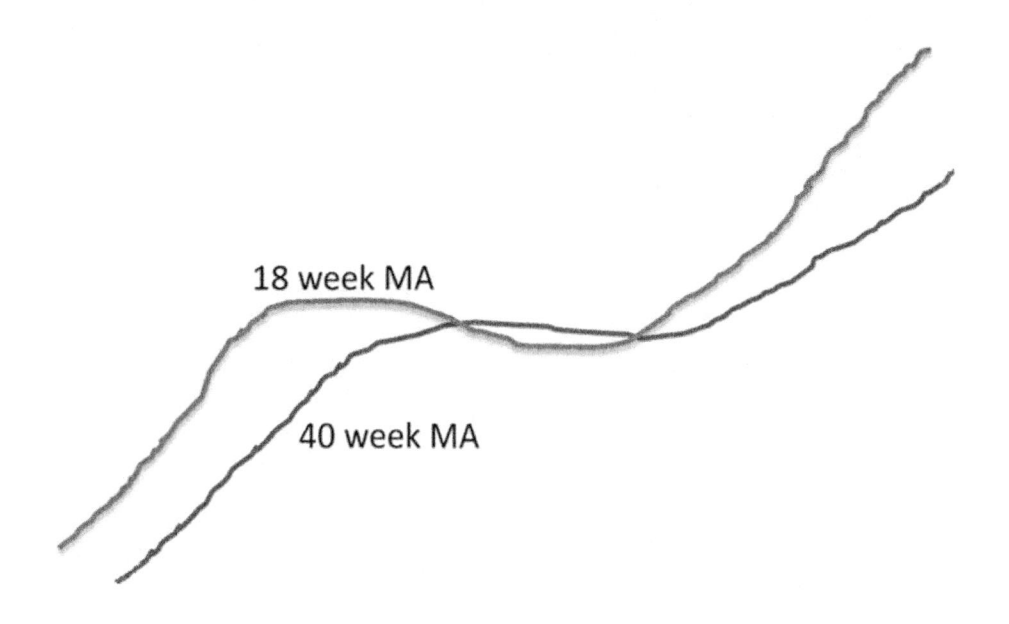

THE TWO GRAPHS ON THIS PAGE SHOW WHAT IS NECESSARY FOR A SETUP TO TAKE PLACE ON THE WEEKLY CHART (LOWER TIME FRAME). THE 18 WEEK MA LINE NEEDS TO CORRECT LONG ENOUGH TO CAUSE IT TO CROSS BELOW THE 40 WEEK LINE (AS SHOWN ABOVE) OR MEET UP WITH THE 40 WEEK LINE (AS SHOWN BELOW).

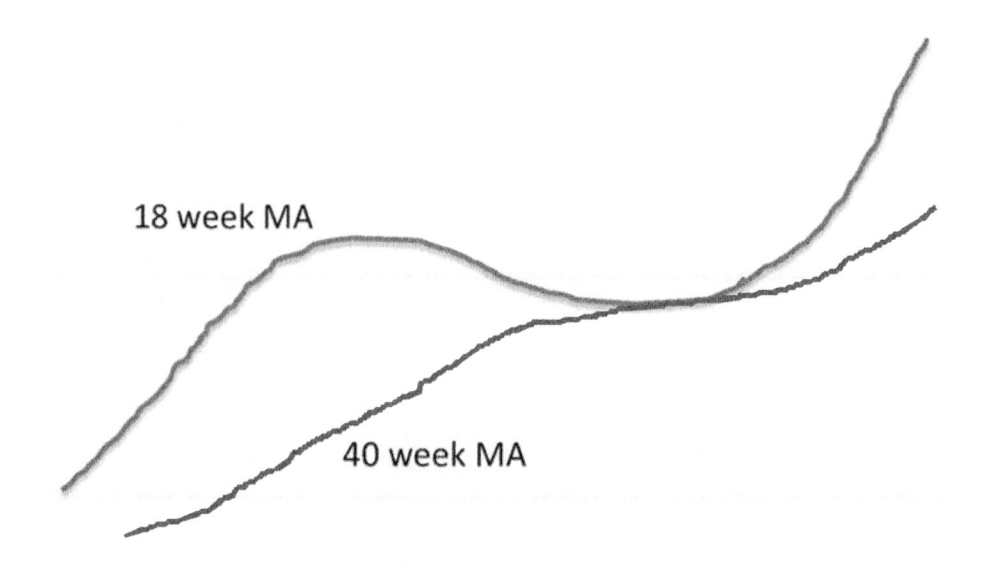

I HAVE OVERLAID THE WEEKLY LINES AND MONTHLY LINES ON THIS GRAPH TO GIVE YOU A BETTER IDEA OF WHAT THIS LOOKS LIKE.

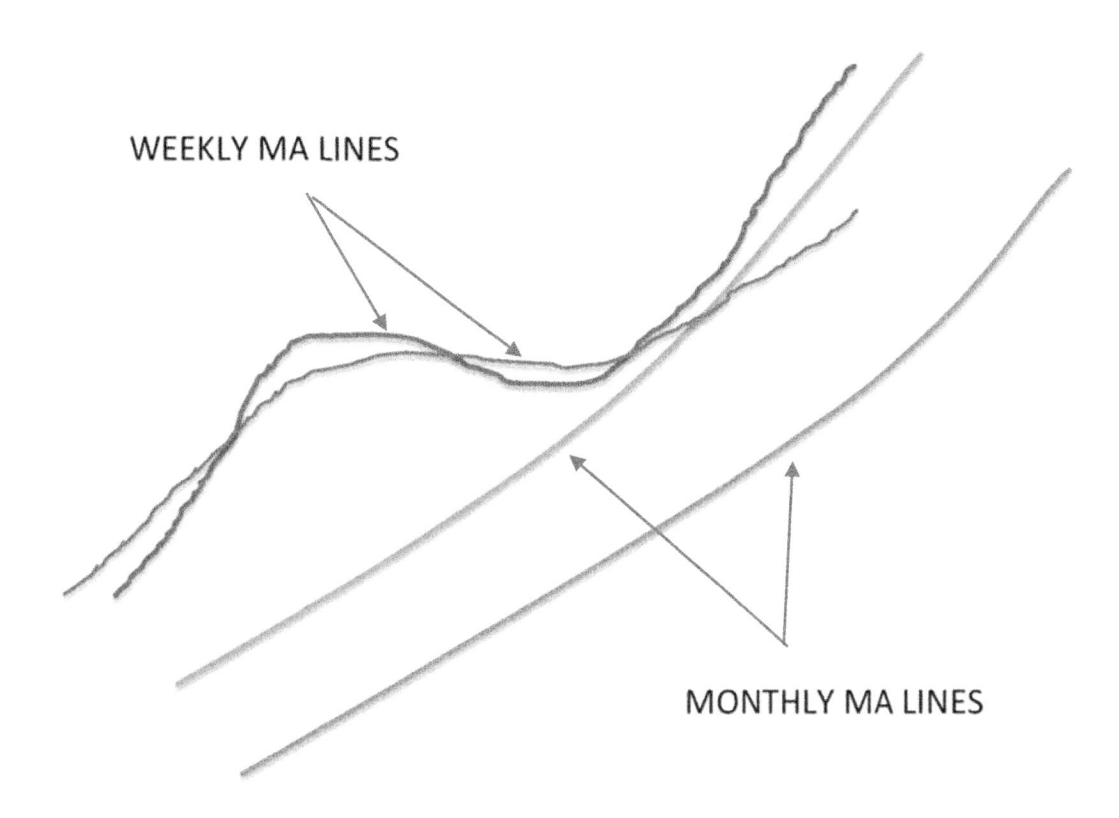

The following pages are examples depicting different versions of this pattern. There are 2 charts per page – monthly and weekly. The monthly chart shows the trend (setup) and the weekly chart is used for entry (trigger) and exit. The monthly trend determines the direction of the trend and therefore helps an investor decide whether to look for long or short signals on the weekly timeframe. Except in very rare circumstances, an investor should never trade counter to the monthly trend. It is important to use momentum indicators such as ADX or Macd to help to determine which stocks have the strongest trends. However, by using the 18 MA and noting its slope as well as how price reacts around this key line, it is possible to determine strong trends using the MA lines by themselves.

Sample Charts

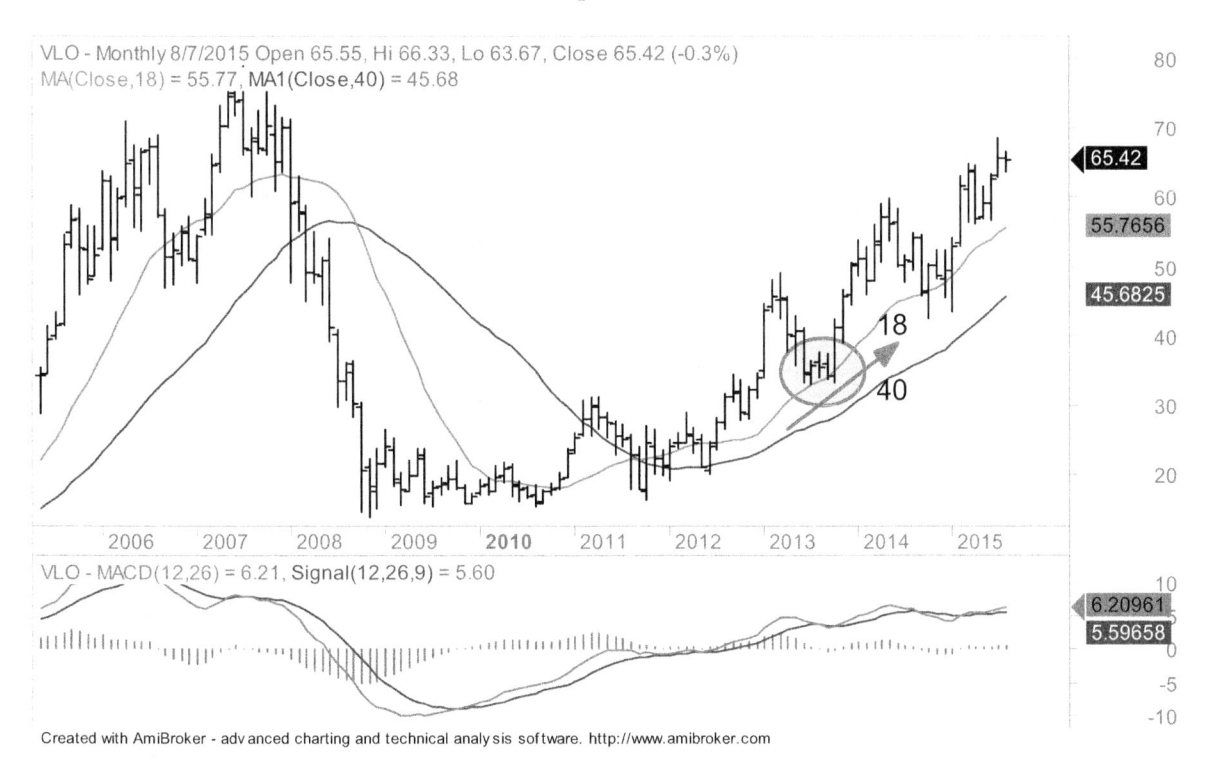

Note the strong slope of the 18 MA on the monthly chart above.

Confirming entry is a break of 40-week MA line which is a 'sell signal that fails.'

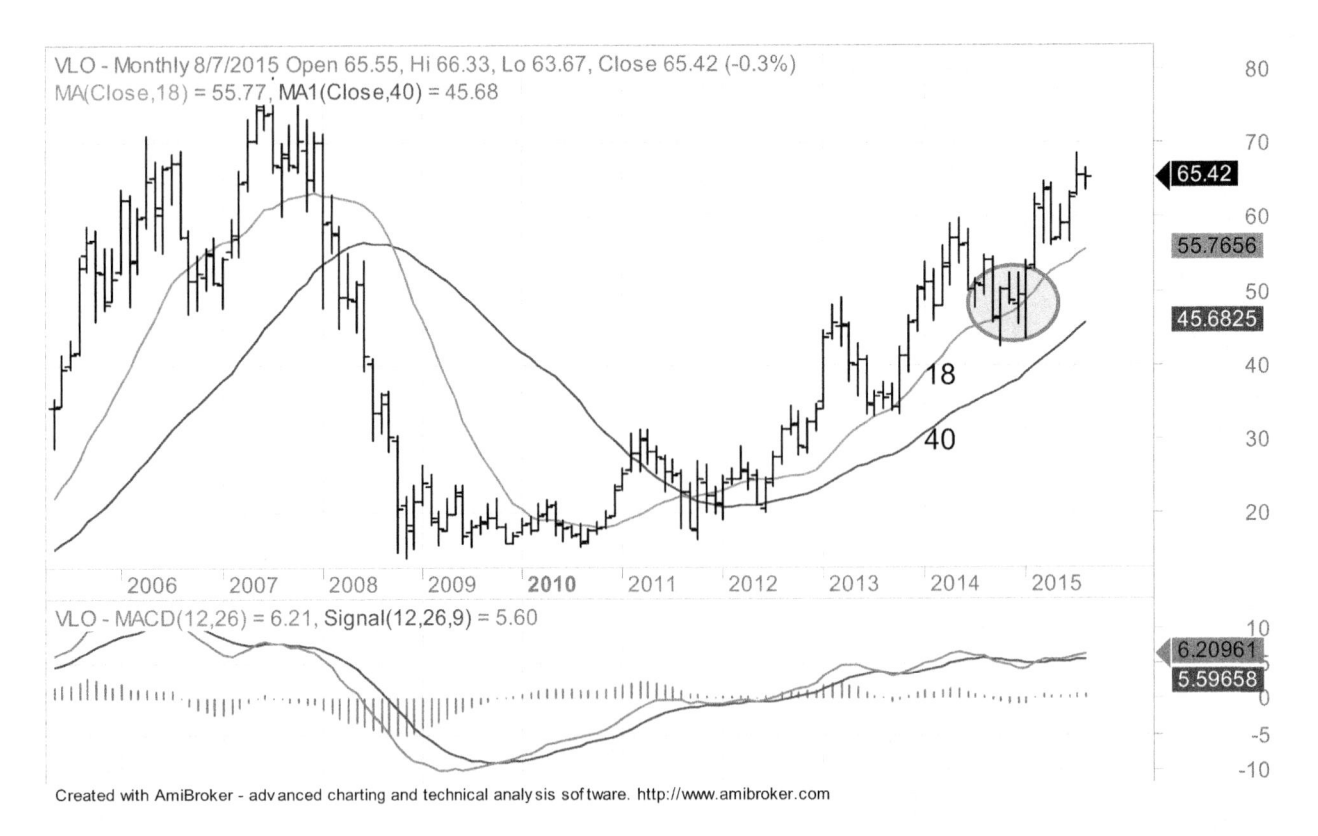

Then it happens again in 2014. Oftentimes, the entry signal will coincide with the 1-2-3 change in trend pattern described on pages 28-30. This is a useful tool to help you identify and confirm the proper entry using the 40-week MA.

Same signal developed in AMZN in 2010...

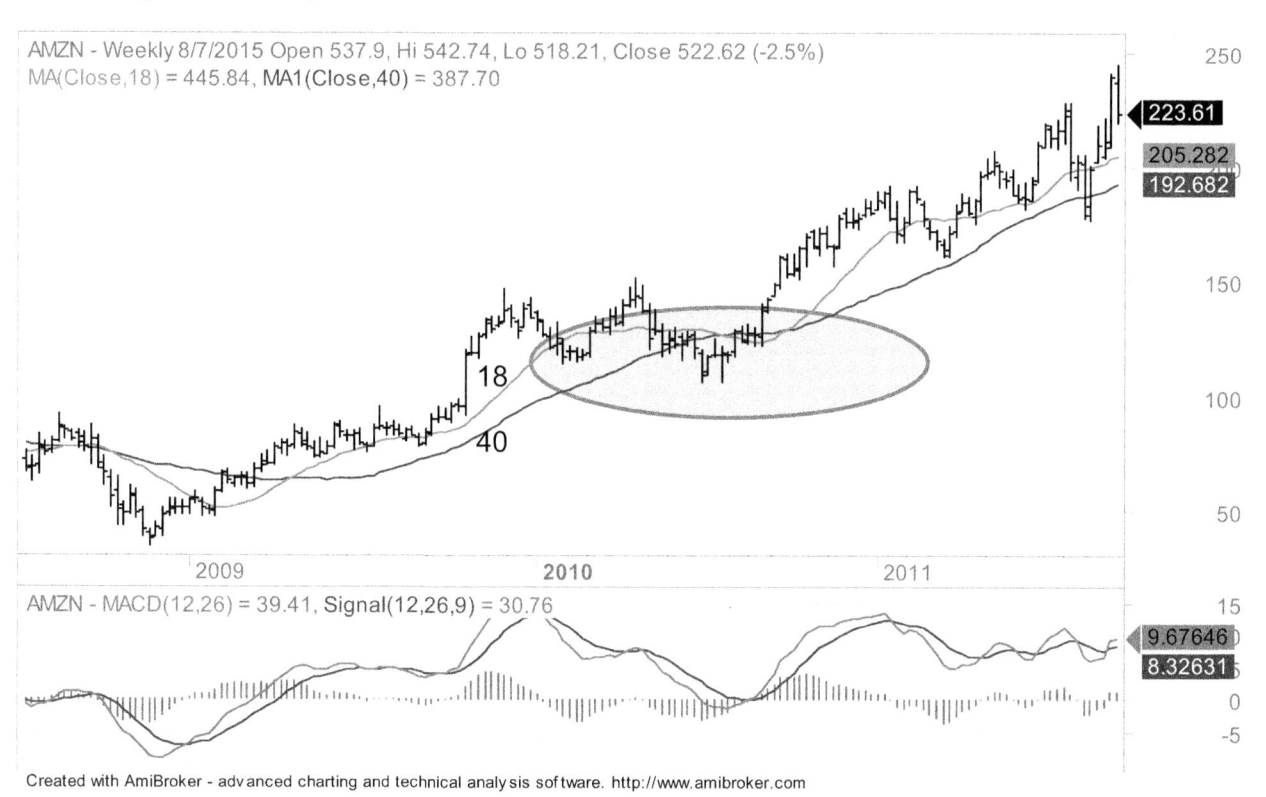

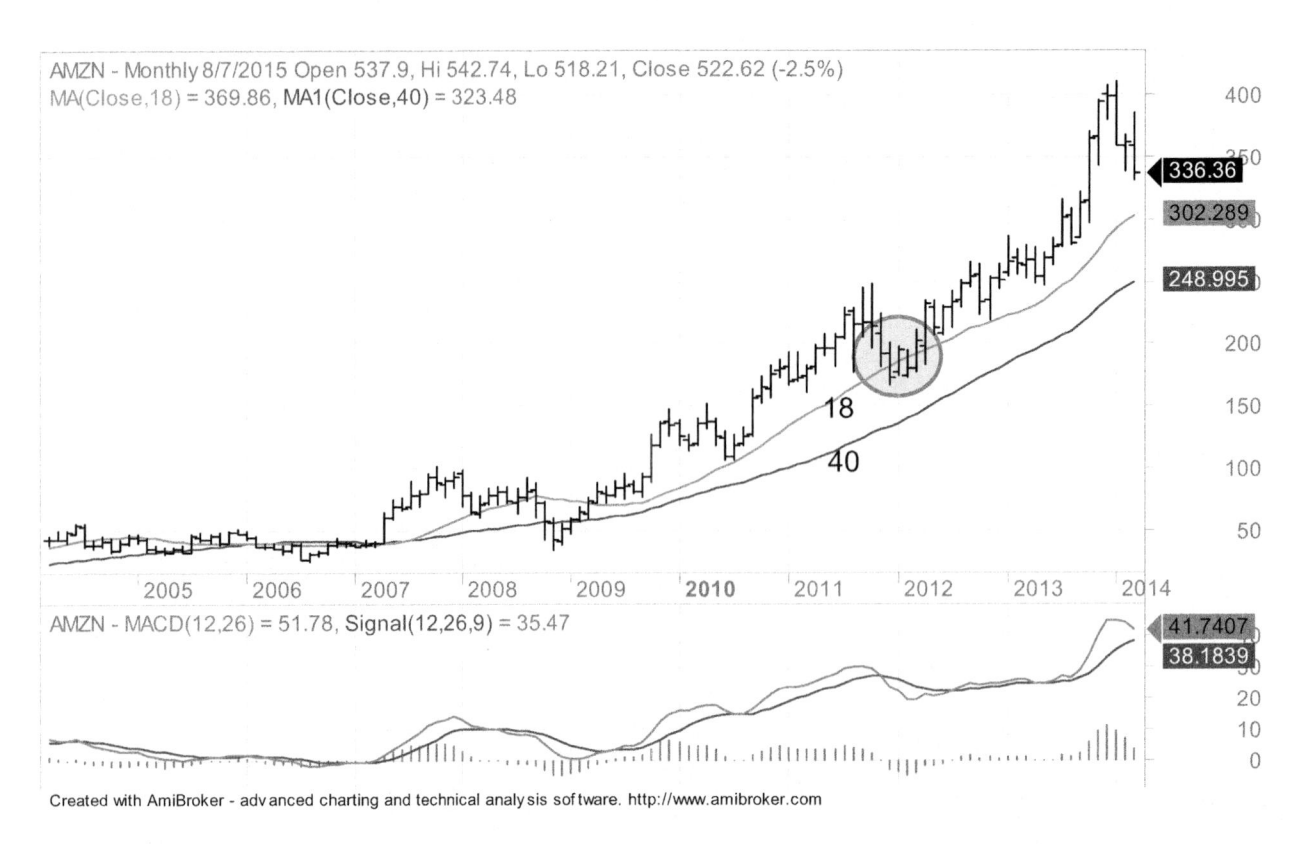

...then again in 2012. Notice the trigger below could have been the first cross of the 40-week MA line in March of 2012. However, by confirming with the 1-2-3 change in trend, the second cross of the 40-week MA in April would have provided a more timely and better reward-to-risk entry.

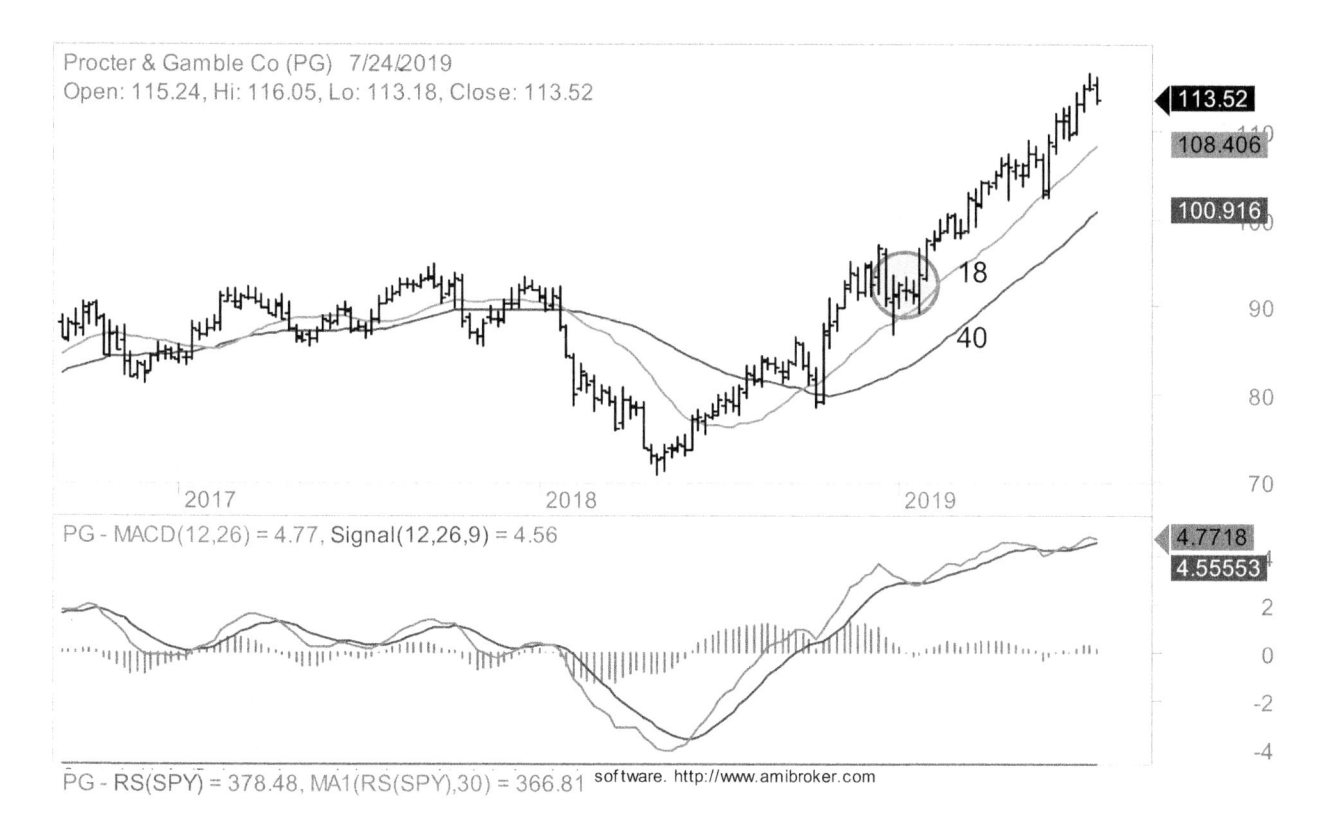

Here is an example of a weekly/daily combination. The weekly chart for PG above has turned positive and is in a strong trend based on the slope of its 18-MA line. Below, the daily chart shows the same pattern of reversal. The entry would have been the higher low that forms after the gap up later in January.

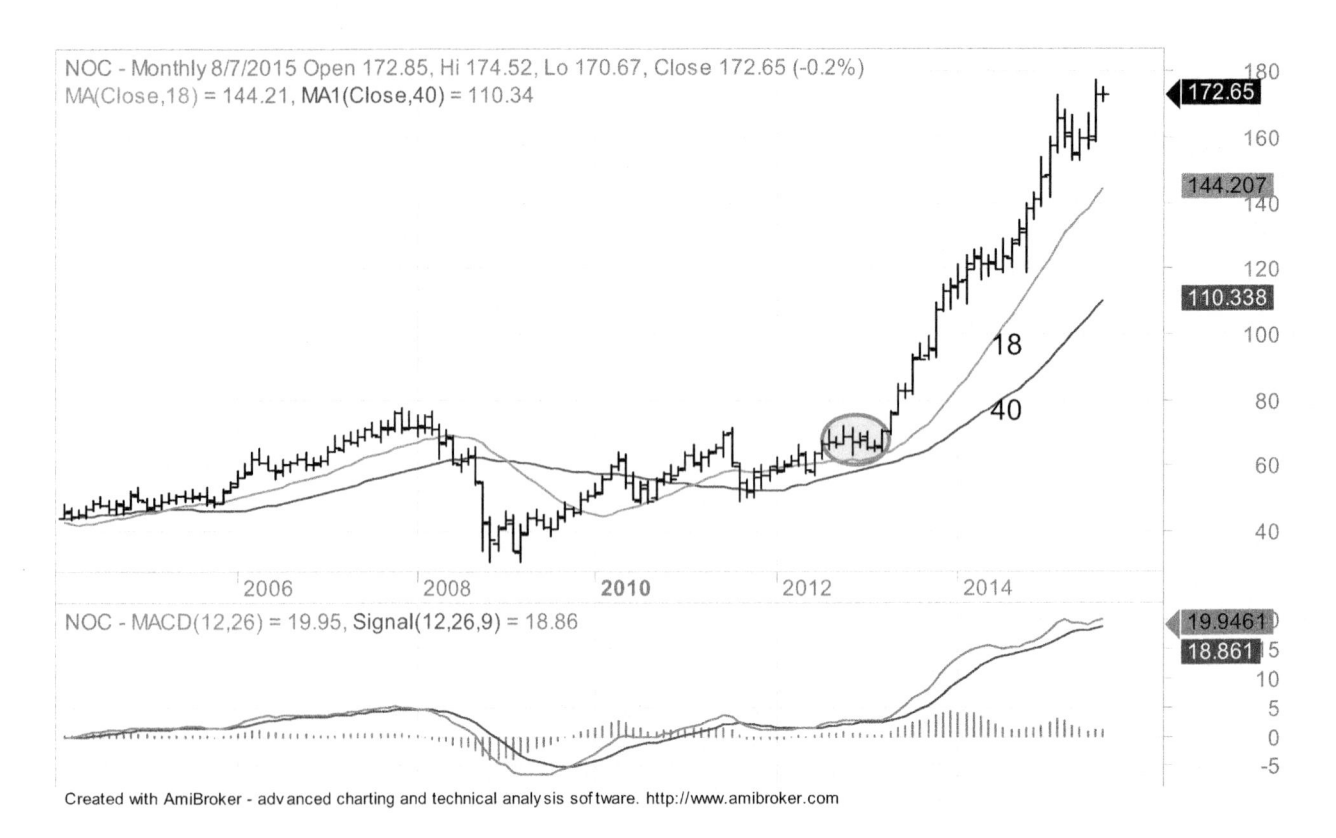

Here is the other type of entry where the 18-week MA does not cross down below the 40-week MA. Instead, they just meet up at the end of March. In this case, we wait for a trendline break.

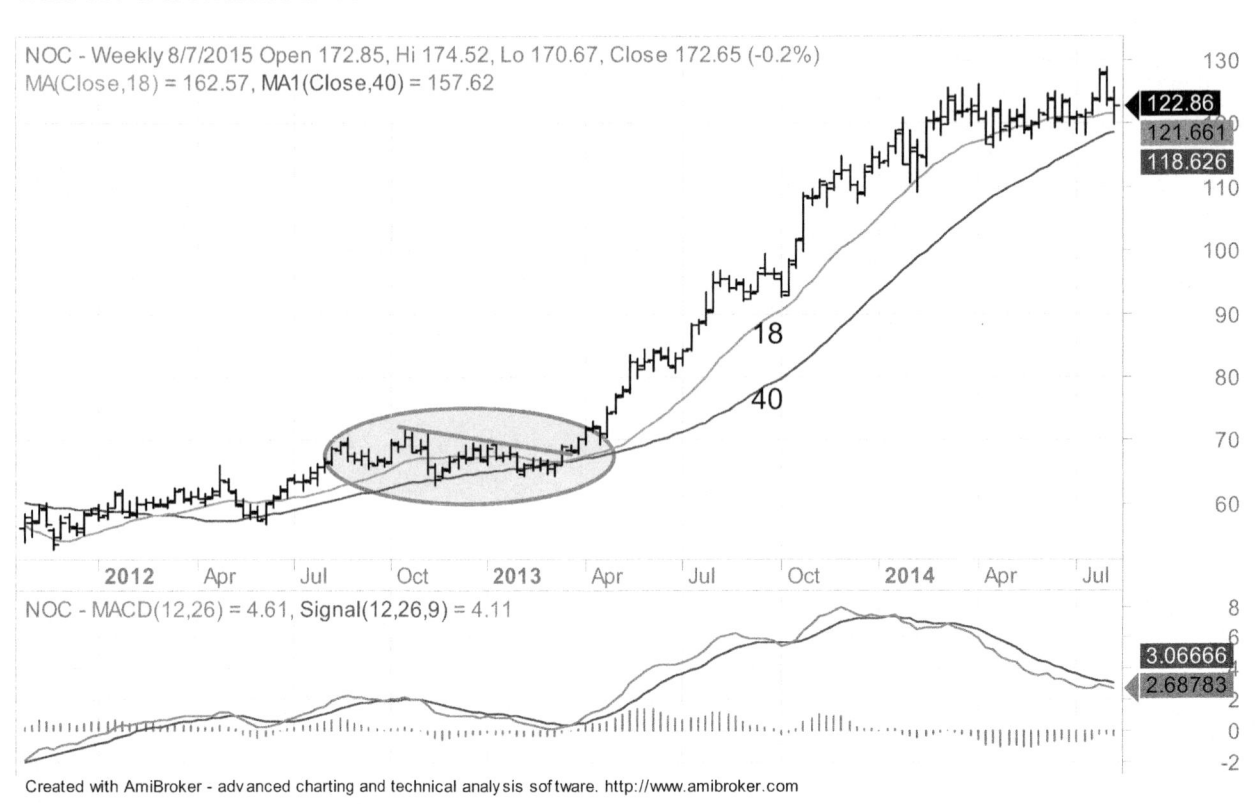

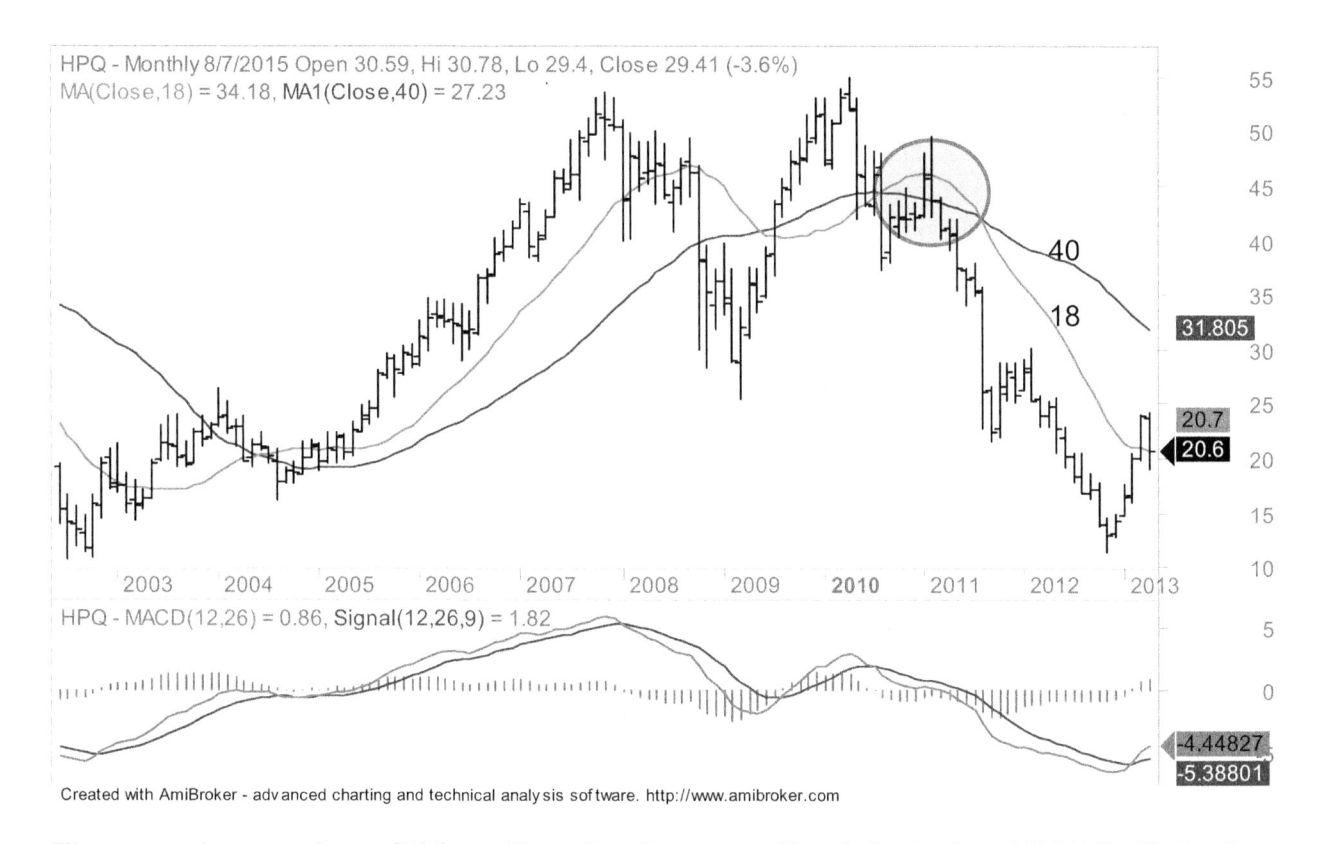

The negative version of this pattern is shown on Hewlett-Packard (HPQ). Entry is the 'buy signal that fails pattern' mentioned several times. Notice how this entry coincides with the trendline break or you could have waited for the mini Step 2 in a change of trend which occurred immediately afterward.

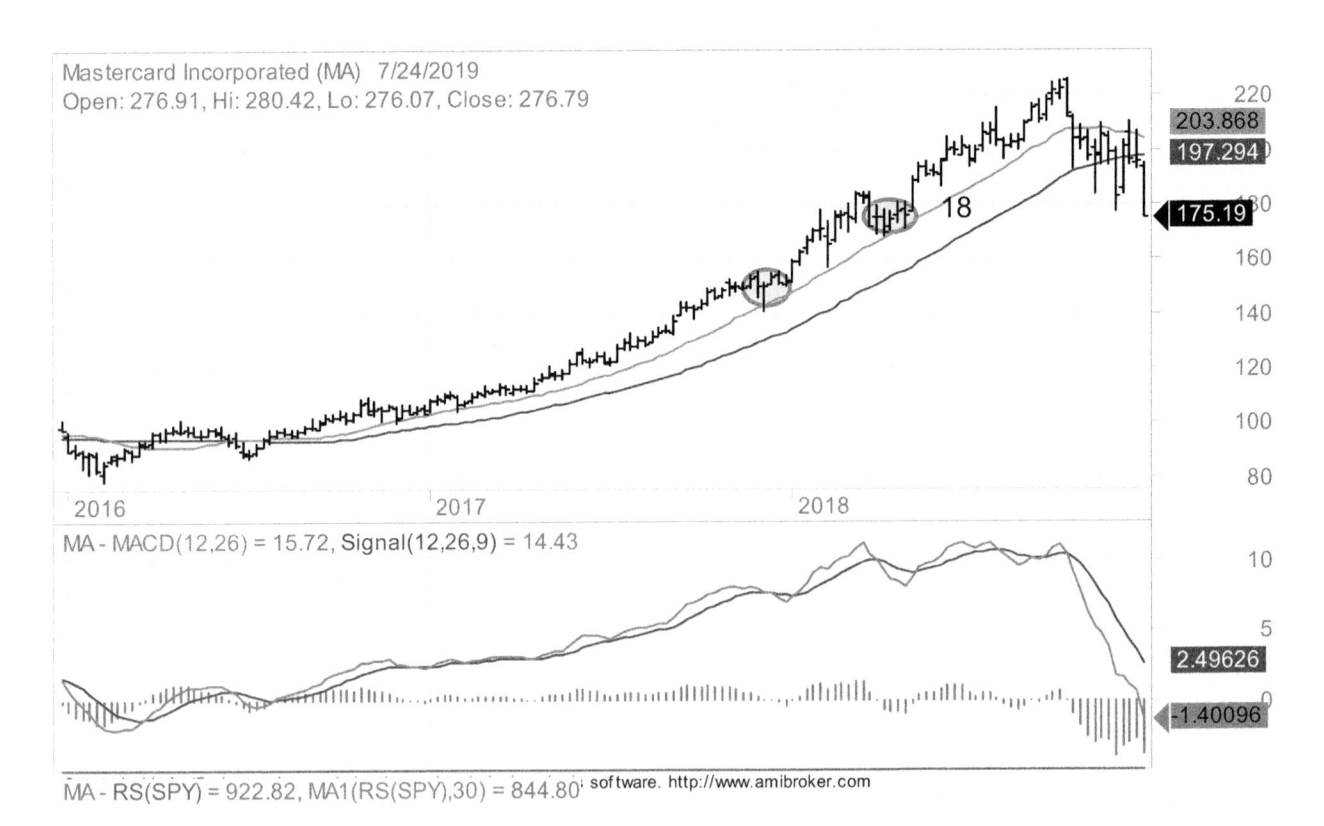

This example of MA shows a strong weekly trend with two chances to enter on the daily chart but with different triggers. The first showed the 18-day MA only pulled back to the 40-day MA, and as a result, entry is the break of the downtrend. The second was our 1-2-3 trend change with 2 being the optimum reward-to-risk entry.

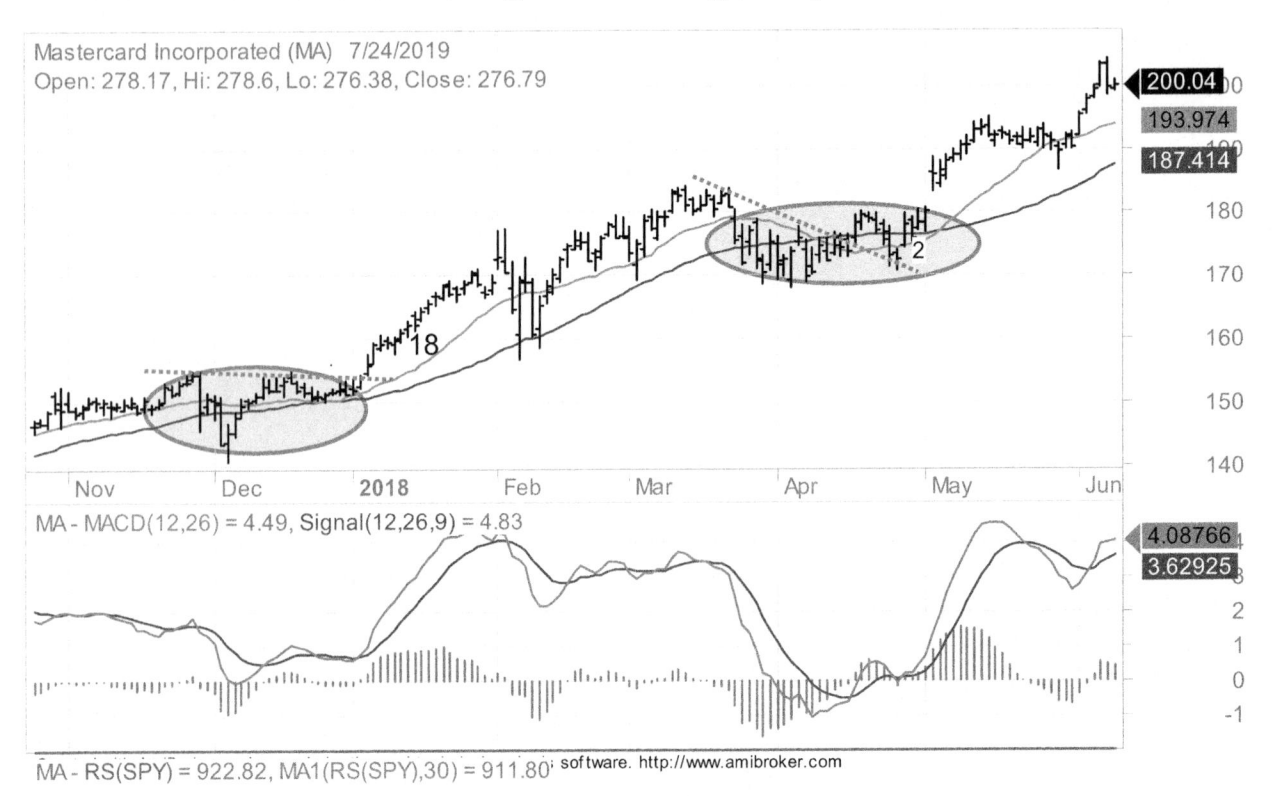

71

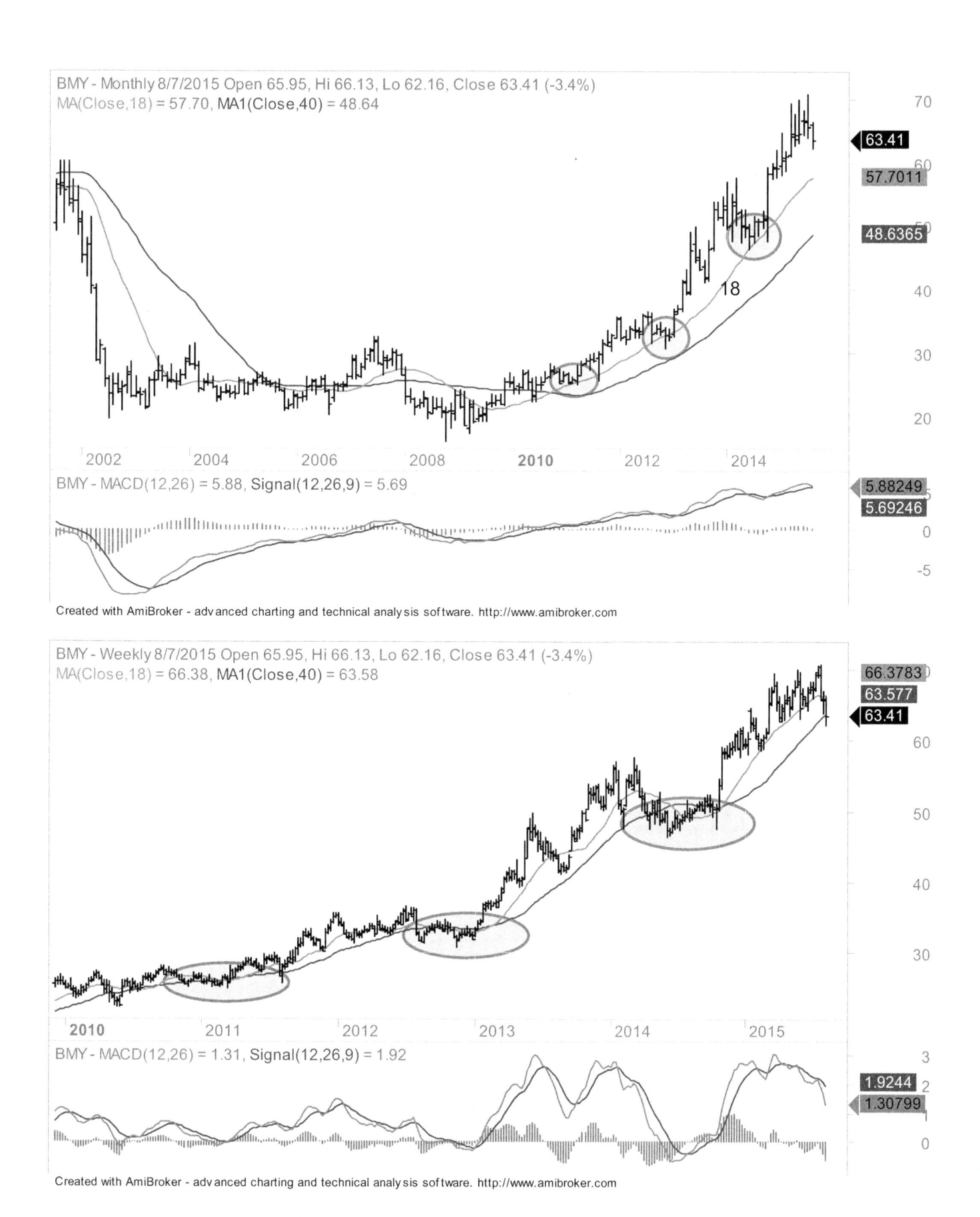

The charts of Bristol-Myers Squibb (BMY) are above. This pattern played out a number of times over the course of several years during the long bull trend for the stock.

WARNING: Do not trade this setup when higher time frame is in a trading range, i.e. not making higher highs and higher lows (long). MA lines may give false signals when there is no trend in place. Waiting for slope to the MA lines on the higher time frame will certainly help but make sure price is trending as well.

All types of trading instruments can be viewed in this manner. The chart below is an intraday chart of the E-Mini for the S&P 500 Contract. Trend reversals and trend strength can be viewed in all time frames with similar tactics. Again, if we take the name, time frame, time info off the chart, the chartist is left with a price chart. As mentioned previously, a chart is a chart.

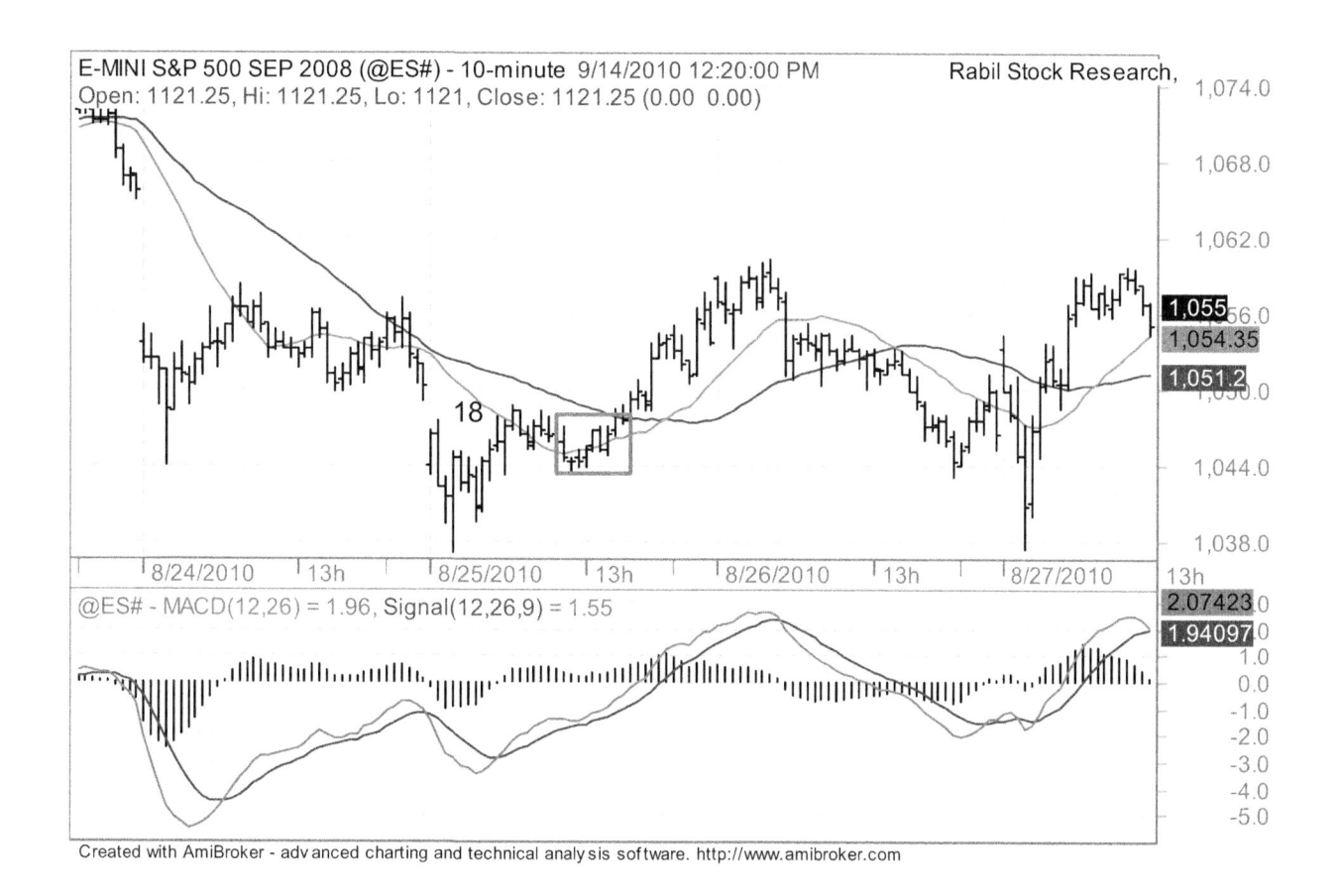

E-Mini S&P 500 (ES) – 10 Minute Chart

The box highlights where the 18 MA on the 10-minute chart changed from falling to rising in the middle of the day on August 25, 2010. This meant there was a change in trend developing based on this particular time frame. A trend on a 10-minute chart can last a few hours to a few days.

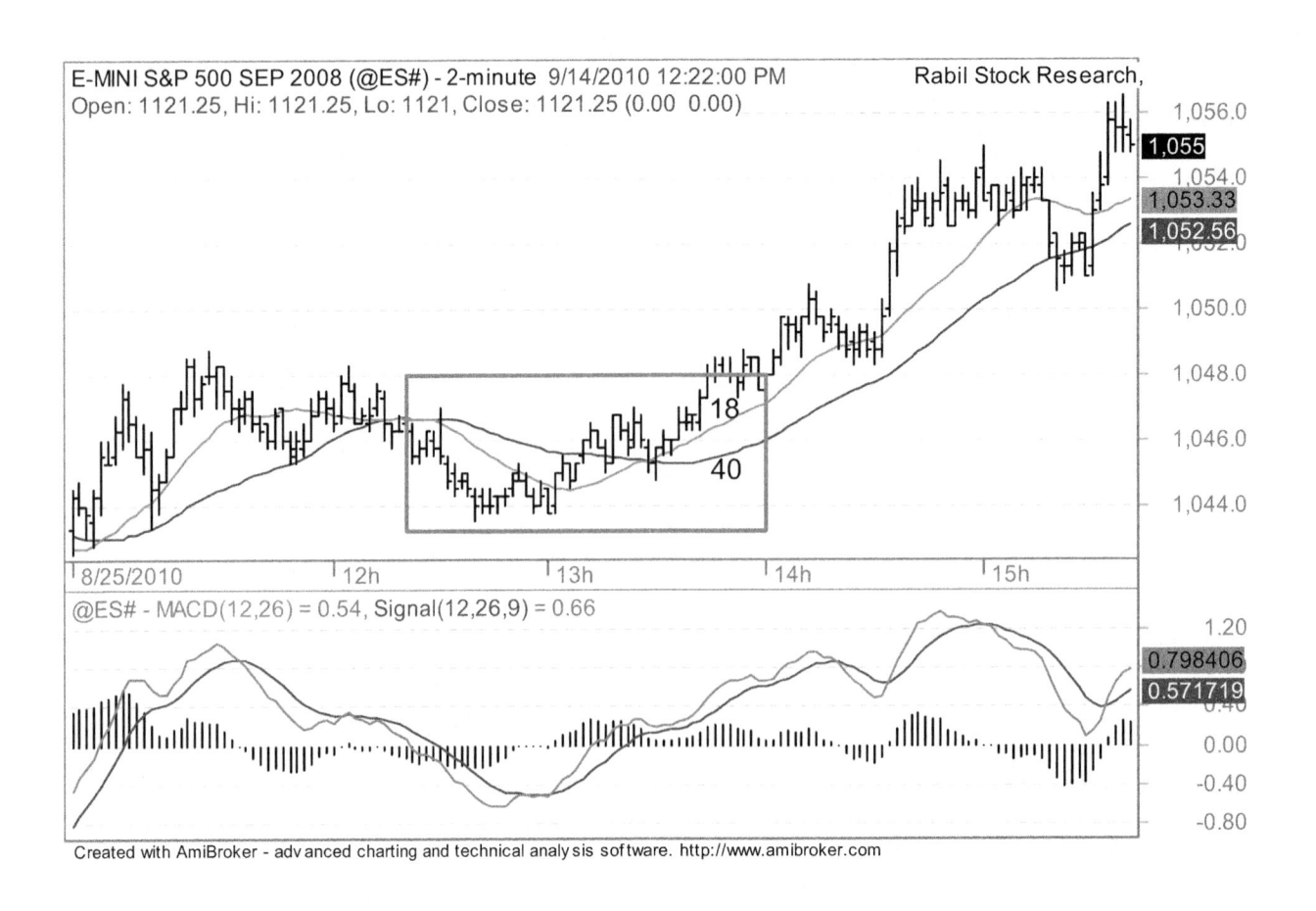

E-Mini S&P 500 (ES) – 2 Minute Chart

The same box shows up on this 2 minute chart on August 25. By using the moving average lines on this 2 minute chart to tell us when to enter, our timing and accuracy can improve dramatically. In this example, the entry trigger would have been the classic buy signal around 1:30pm. These types of trades are taking place all day every day by professional traders in the E-Mini S&P contract. The most important part of this strategy is understanding that the direction is determined by the 10 minute chart or the longer time frame. Then, once direction, up or down, is determined, the 2 minute time frame helps us pinpoint our entry point.

The exact strategy described above using the E-Mini S&P 500 contract can be applied to individual stocks on intraday time frames as well as longer term Monthly, Weekly and Daily time frames. The important thing to keep in mind is that the smaller the time frame, the less reliable the signal, especially on smaller intraday time frames when there is excessive intraday market volatility.

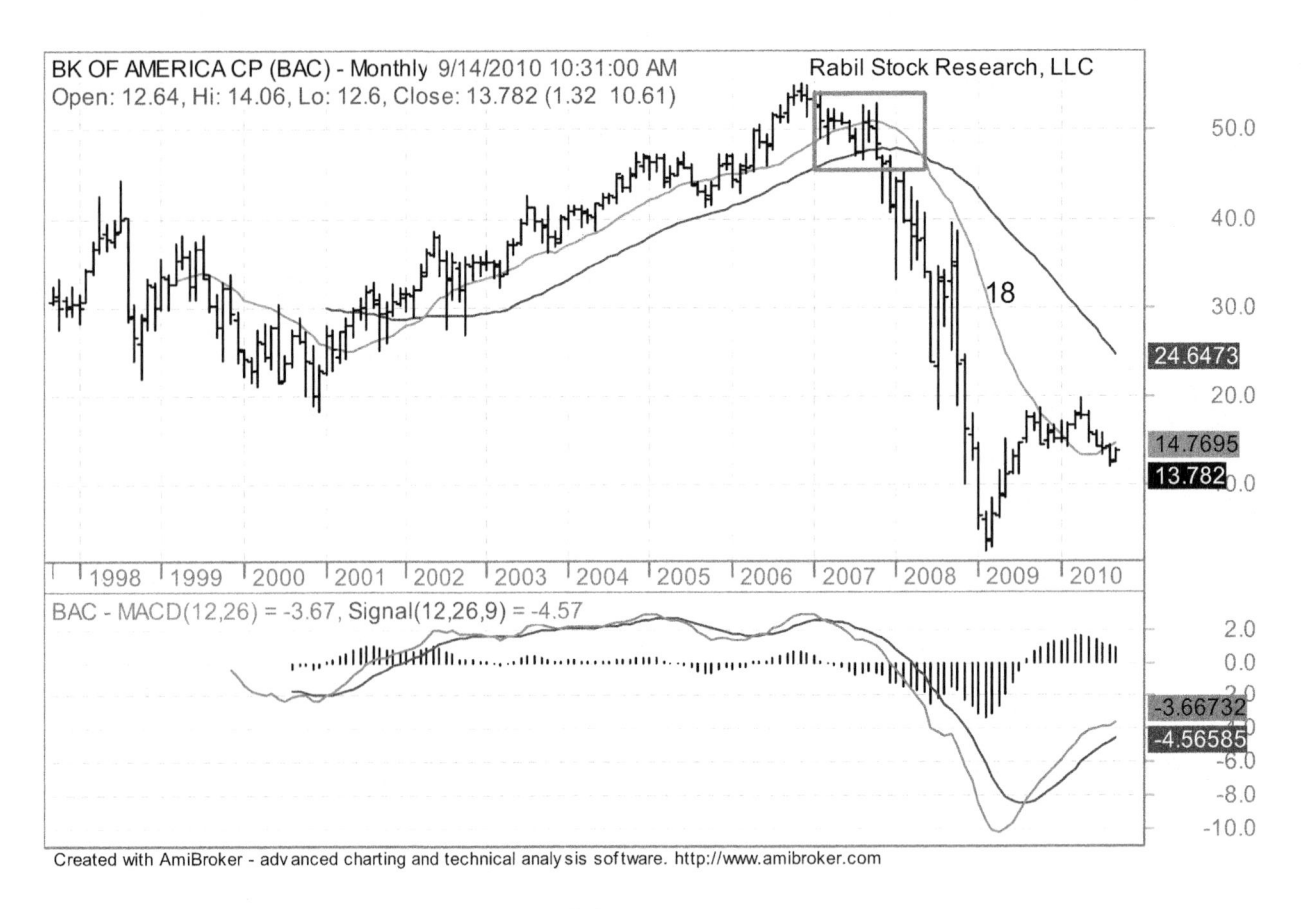

Bank of America (BAC) – Monthly

The slope of the 18 MA on the Monthly chart above was rising from early 2001 until late 2007. Once this line started to roll over, the long-term trend took a turn for the worse.

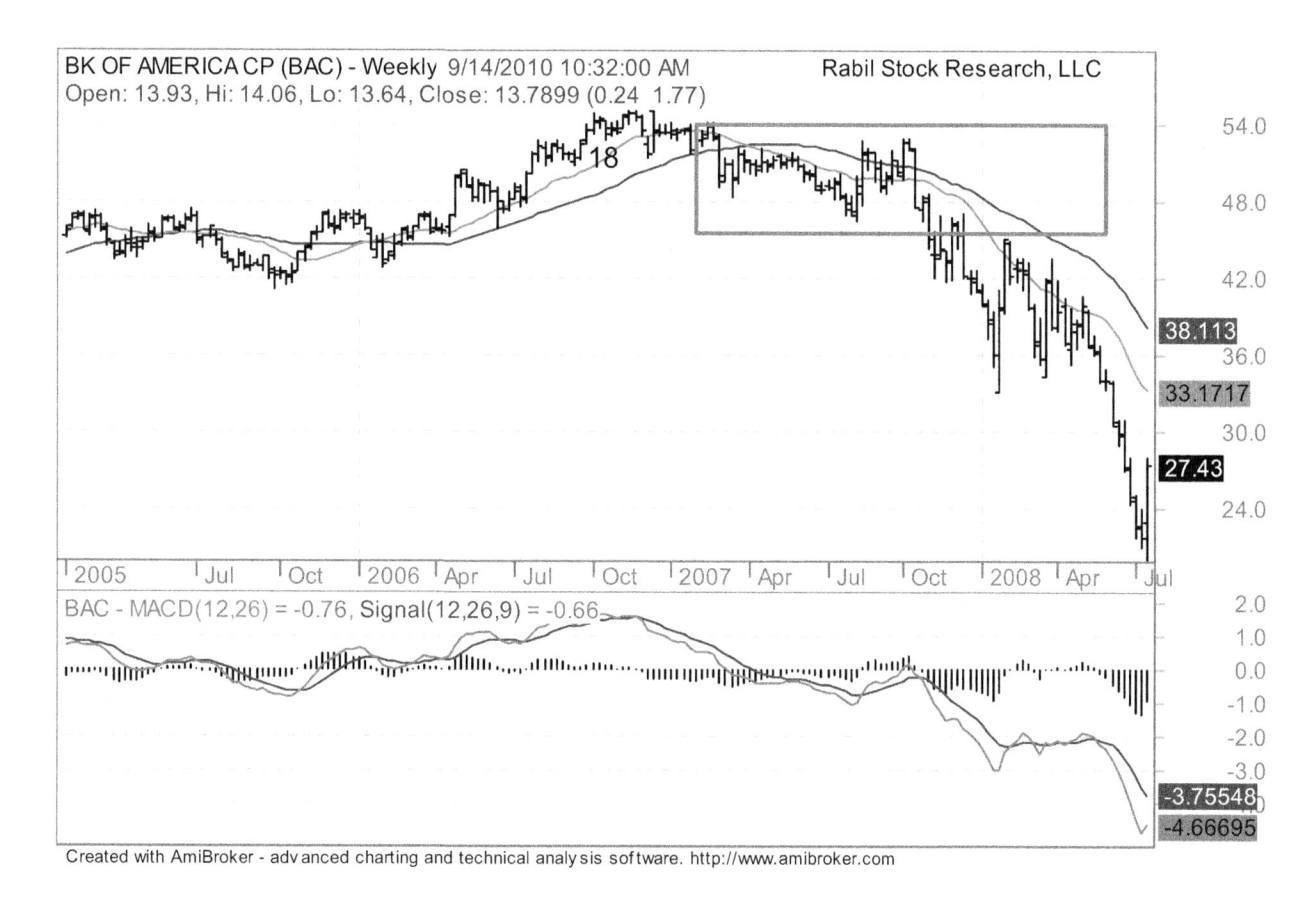

Bank of America (BAC) - Weekly

The box on this Weekly chart shows where the 18 Monthly MA started to roll over. The actual point was in October 2007. Essentially, this is where the wind starts blowing in your face. It is difficult to make money in this type of environment unless you are looking for short sale opportunities.

We always give more credence to the longer time frame (multiple time frames - Rule 2). For most long-term investors, we recommend using the weekly chart to determine the entry and exits points. The monthly chart, I believe, coincides with the fundamental outlook. I have found that the monthly chart does an excellent job of distinguishing between *corrections* in long term bullish trends and *breaks* in the long-term trends.

In strict terms, the monthly carries more weight than the weekly, and the weekly carries more weight than the daily. Most importantly, when using 2-time frames, always use the longer time frame to determine the trend and the shorter time frame for entry and exits.

As I have said several times, each time frame has its own trend structure. This means that a monthly chart can be in an uptrend while a weekly chart is in a downtrend and a daily chart is in an uptrend. The best combination of trend structure is when the higher time frame is showing early signs of a change in trend and the lower time frame is confirming a change in the same direction. This offers investors the best opportunity to get into new trends early.

Using the MACD Indicator in Conjunction with the Moving Average Signals

MACD stands for moving average convergence divergence. This indicator has been one of the most popular indicators for the past few decades. MACD is a momentum indicator and can be useful for determining the strength of a given trend, overbought and oversold conditions as well as imminent reversal areas.

In basic terms, MACD plots the difference between two moving average lines. The creator of the indicator, Gerald Appel, used exponential moving averages in his calculation. The popular EMA lines used are 12 (fast) and 26 (slow) and the difference between these lines is displayed as the actual MACD line. In addition, this indicator employs a Signal line, which is a moving average of the MACD line, in this case a 9 EMA.

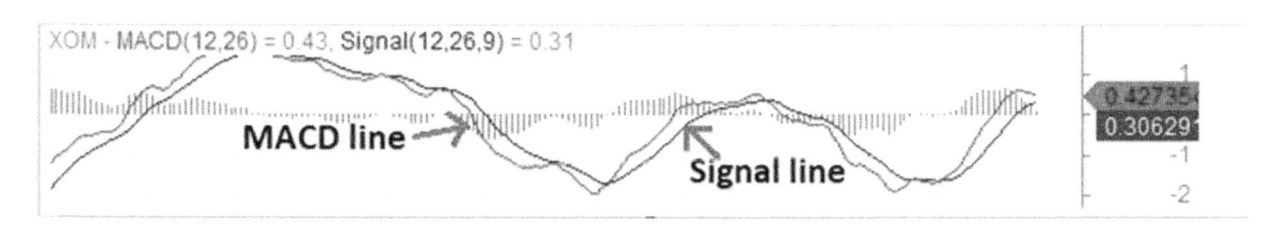

I have always used the original MACD settings in my work with clients over the past 30 years. MACD was the first indicator I used when I started in technical analysis and has continued to play a role in my interpretations of the trend and its strength. An important factor is that since MACD is based on MA lines, it is calculated using the closing price of a stock. The high and low range for each bar is completely ignored. This fact will become more significant when I explain the use of the ADX indicator in the next chapter.

If you browse through the example charts in the previous section, you will notice MACD is in the lower scale on every one of the charts. There are specific signals and characteristics I look for when using this indicator in conjunction with the 18 MA and 40 MA lines. I am sure you are wondering how a 12/26 EMA indicator would work with 18/40 SMA lines. Keep in mind, the idea is to use the methods independently and then look for common ground. I have purposely not spoken about any indicators up until this point. The reason, as I stated earlier, is that you must become proficient at reading price patterns, trends and structure without the use of indicators before moving on. It is critical that you develop the skill of seeing the trend and change of trend, preferably with only price bars on the chart. Then, it becomes useful to use indicators to improve and enhance what you are already seeing with the price action. To repeat, start with price bars, then add MA lines, followed by using the MACD or ADX or both.

There are specific patterns that develop with MACD that I am going to cover with numerous examples. The four most prominent signals for my work are zero line reversals, pinch plays, momentum divergence and reverse divergence.

Zero Line Reversals

With the MACD indicator, the zero level is where the fast moving line (12) crosses the slowing moving line (26). In the chart below, I have added a 12 EMA and 26 EMA to the price chart so you can understand the calculation. As I have mentioned previously, I do not use MA crossover signals as operative buy/sell signals, but they are useful at helping to define the trend. So, the zero line (highlighted in lower scale with horizontal line)

signifies the level where these two EMA lines meet and cross one another. Oftentimes, good signals take place near this level. The chart below is the same daily chart of Herbalife (HLF) only with the 18 and 40 simple MA lines back with the price chart.

Notice that in February, MACD crossed down through the zero line at almost the exact same time that price broke its trendline. This is the start of the change of trend sequence and the rally back in March sets up the classic sell signal following the 18 and 40 MA line crossover to the downside. Zero line reversal signals take place when the MACD line itself rallies back toward that key level and turns down. The is a great example because it shows the power of having confluence amongst the price structure (1-2-3 change in trend), the MA pattern (classic sell signal) and the failure of the MACD line near its zero level. When you can build a case with independent signals, your odds will improve.

The daily chart of Delek US Holdings Inc. (DK) above shows the zero line reversal in a different form. This rally toward zero signifies the counter trend rally on this time frame vs the downtrend on the higher time frame (weekly). Notice the 1-2-3

sequence that takes place as well as the 'buy signal that fails' using the 18 and 40 MA lines. MACD crossing down through its Signal line is the operative sell signal here and gives the investor a great timing tool to use in conjunction with the other indicators. I cannot stress enough the skill of recognizing the price structure together with the MA setups to give you the understanding of where a stock is situated in its price trend. Then, adding the MACD will improve the timing and confidence even more.

The chart of Sysco Corp. (SYY) is another example of a zero line reversal which helps with the timing of a lower time frame entry. The arrow points out the actual MACD cross of the Signal line following the zero line reversal.

Now, I suggest going back through the charts from the previous section and notices how many of the lower time frame signals are zero line reversals.

Pinch Plays

Linda Raschke wrote a book called "Street Smarts" with Larry Connors. This is a great book. One of their signals is called an 'Anti'. They use a different form of MACD or Stochastic to find this signal. However, the concept is the same. We want to find when the Signal line has turned or is trending and the MACD moves counter to it. It causes the two lines to pinch together for a brief period without causing a crossover. The weekly chart of Apple Inc. (AAPL) from 1999 shows back to back Pinch signals after price emerged out of its base. Typically, price will pullback 2-3 bars or will drift sideways to alleviate the short term overbought condition.

Sometimes these signals will take place following momentum divergence (discussed next) or in conjunction with divergence patterns. Once again, the best signals will usually emerge when there are signals from the price structure and the MA lines to confirm.

The chart of Pepsico Inc. (PEP) from 2018 is above. Price breaks the trendline (step 1) and then tests (step 2). This process is also the 40 to 18 bounce pattern discussed prior. During this rally to the 18 MA line, MACD is unable to regain its Signal line causing a minor pinch to develop. This gives us enough evidence to sell as soon as 18 MA line is re-broken instead of waiting for step 3 or the break of the 40 MA line. One of the keys to this signal is watching the price action. Many times, the MACD line will only tighten to the Signal line slightly so focusing on the counter trend move in price helps this pattern to become easier to recognize. In addition, the first two pinch plays are the highest probability and then the odds start to drop off somewhat due to the longevity of the trend. In this example, the reward to risk improves dramatically using this entry trigger rather than waiting.

I have a Pinch Play trading plan that I describe in detail later in the manual.

Momentum Divergence

Let's use the same chart of PEP just prior to the downside pinch signal in December. Price made the highest high on the chart at the end of November but notice what happened to the MACD line. For the first time in this uptrend, the line did not hit a new high with price. This is referred to bearish momentum divergence.

(I also highlighted two other nice Pinch Play setups – arrows). The momentum divergence signal means the momentum is slowing down. In other words, the fast (12) line is starting to rise at a slower rate than the slow (26) line. As a result, the difference between the two line begins to shrink. This can be used as an exit signal for an existing holding. In addition, it can provide an early entry point during a pullback on the lower time frame when the higher time frame trend remains strong.

Microsoft Corp. (MSFT) monthly shows bullish conditions with the 18 MA and 40 MA rising together at about the same rate, almost parallel. This is representative of a strong trend in 2014-2015 (circled area).

The weekly chart above shows the MACD divergence that takes place in the circled area during the 2015 correction phase. Using the two time frames together this way will allow you to anticipate this type of signal as it is pulling back.

Momentum divergence used as a signal counter to a strong trend on the higher time frame will not be as reliable. Also, this kind of momentum divergence has been misconstrued by many investors. This type of divergence does not necessarily mean a reversal in the trend is coming. In most cases, this signal will drop the stock to prior support or rally it toward prior resistance depending on whether it is bearish or bullish. We typically want to focus our efforts on using this divergence pattern in the direction of the higher time frame and not against it.

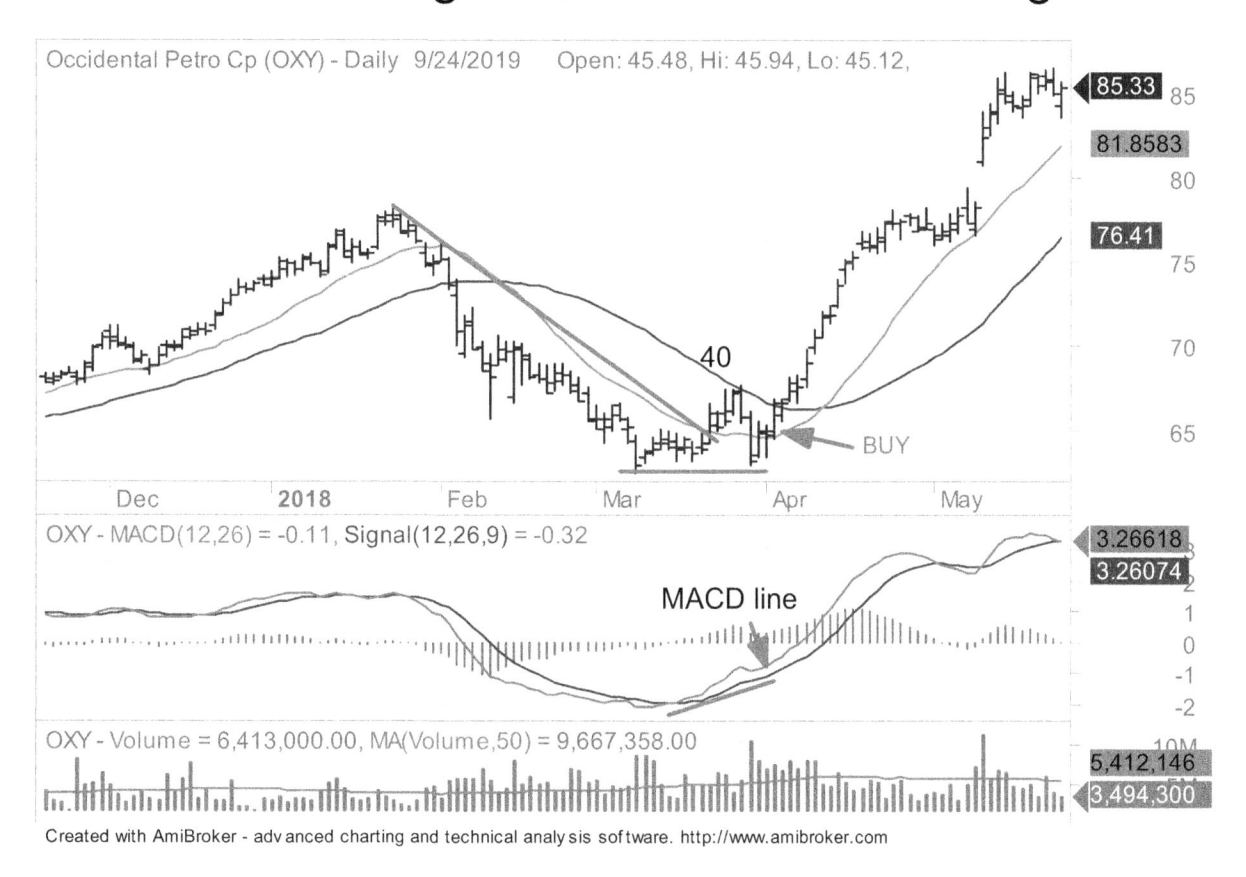

The daily chart of Occidental Petro Corp. (OXY) is above. This is a great example and combines the 1-2-3 change of trend sequence and the 40 to 18 bounce pattern with a different form of bullish momentum divergence. Note that price essentially makes a double bottom (step 2). Instead of testing with price, MACD makes a significantly higher low. This still qualifies as divergence in my view since the momentum is so much stronger than price. In addition, notice the pinch play that developed at this bottom. This would have offered a great opportunity to enter a potential trend reversal with a better trigger by combining the MACD with the MA pattern.

Ollie' Bargain Outlet (OLLI) provides another example of the 'divergent pinch play' on the negative side. This signal takes place when MACD displays a momentum divergence and a pinch play at the same time. This is a good pattern and this bearish signal is one to watch in your holdings for an excellent early exit signal or it can be used as previously described as an early entry trigger into the higher time frame trend.

Reverse Divergence

Standard MACD bullish divergence, as just discussed, takes place when price makes a lower low and MACD makes a higher low. Bullish reverse divergence is when price makes a higher low and MACD makes a lower low.

The chart of UnitedHealth Group (UNH) is above. Notice that price pulls back at the end of June and makes a higher bottom than the bottom in May. At the same time, the MACD line makes a significantly lower low. This type of bullish signal takes place when the MACD are not in a smooth trend and the

MACD lines continually crosses down through the Signal line on each pullback or correction. To improve the probability of this pattern, look for it earlier in the trend rather than later. Also, we want to see price find support at either the 18 MA or the 40 MA line for this pattern. In the case of UNH, price reversed at the 40-day MA line.

The hourly chart of INTC shows a reverse divergence which finds support at the 18 MA line.

This type of divergence needs to be monitored more closely after entry since standard divergence or the pinch pattern can develop after this signal if the resulting move is not strong enough.

Above, Proctor & Gamble Co. (PG) shows two back to back bearish versions of this signals. The first signal takes place at the 18-day MA and the second at the 40-day MA line. Notice, that if you were looking at MACD by itself, you may have considered this a bullish looking pattern and missed the bigger trend. Remember, standard divergence only suggests a decline or rally (in this case) to prior resistance.

When to Use the Crossover versus the Pinch

Price is always the preferred entry trigger over an indicator. Any indicator is a derivative of price so there is almost always some lag. As a result, we should focus our entry signals using price whenever possible. However, some ideas will come via a screen or filter, so we need to know the difference between timely crosses of the Signal line and higher risk crosses. The chart of Citizens Financial Group (CFG) is below. The cross is circled and notice that the day of the trigger was the third day up in the pattern. This is a high risk trigger since the stock has already moved 3-4 days in the sequence.

TD Ameritrade (AMTD) shows a timely MACD cross signal. The first day of the move was also a cross of the 18-day MA line. Typically, the low risk triggers will take place when the price bar on the cross day is still touching the 18 MA line. However, if you track the number of days a stock has risen on the day of the trigger, you will recognize when it is better to wait for a pinch setup. In the case of CFG, the pinch took place about a week later.

Putting it together:
Multiple time frames and MACD

The monthly chart of Visa Inc. (V) provides the starting point for analyzing a stock we would like to potentially invest in for a longer term trade. Notice the clear pattern of higher highs and lows on this chart from lower left to upper right. In addition, the slope of the MA lines remains strong and consistent with a comfortable distance between them. The circled area shows the 18-month MA is rising at a slightly faster rate than the 40-month MA line but not significantly so. This is a solid trend on the higher time frame and the pullback to the 18-month MA line in late 2018 was the first in nearly two years.

At this point, we want to move down to the weekly time frame (below). The same circle is showing on this time frame. Price has corrected enough on the weekly chart to cause the 18-week MA line to come down and meet up with the 40-week MA in early 2019. MACD has formed a zero line reversal. The week of the MACD crossover is the same week the price chart broke its trendline.

This provides an excellent example of how MACD can be used to confirm the MA setup and to help to pinpoint the proper entry point. Always start with the higher time frame and look for a solid turnaround pattern or a strong trend. Then, move down to the lower time frame and wait for the proper correction and reversal to trigger before making an investment.

Using the ADX indicator

ADX (Average Directional Index) is used to analyze the strength of a trend. It is a complex indicator with several moving parts. An in-depth understanding of how to use this indicator will take time. I am going to provide you with a simple explanation of how it is calculated and how it can be incorporated into what I have already explained.

In the last chapter, the MACD indicator was explained. It uses closing prices in its calculation.

I bring this up again to make the distinction between MACD and ADX as to why they are very different and why they can complement one another.

ADX uses the high/low range to calculate the lines. The closes play no factor at all in this indicator. So, MACD uses the closes and ADX uses the range. This is a critical distinction since the market goes through changes in volatility as much as it goes through changes in trend. When volatility expands, the MACD carries more weight and as volatility contracts, the ADX indicator increases in its importance. You can do fine by picking one or the other but each of these indicators provide outstanding signals at times and I believe it is beneficial to understand both.

ADX Calculation

This is the same monthly chart of Visa Inc. (V) from the last section. I have zoomed in on the last few years to show the +DI (Directional Plus) and the -DI (Directional Minus) and how they are derived.

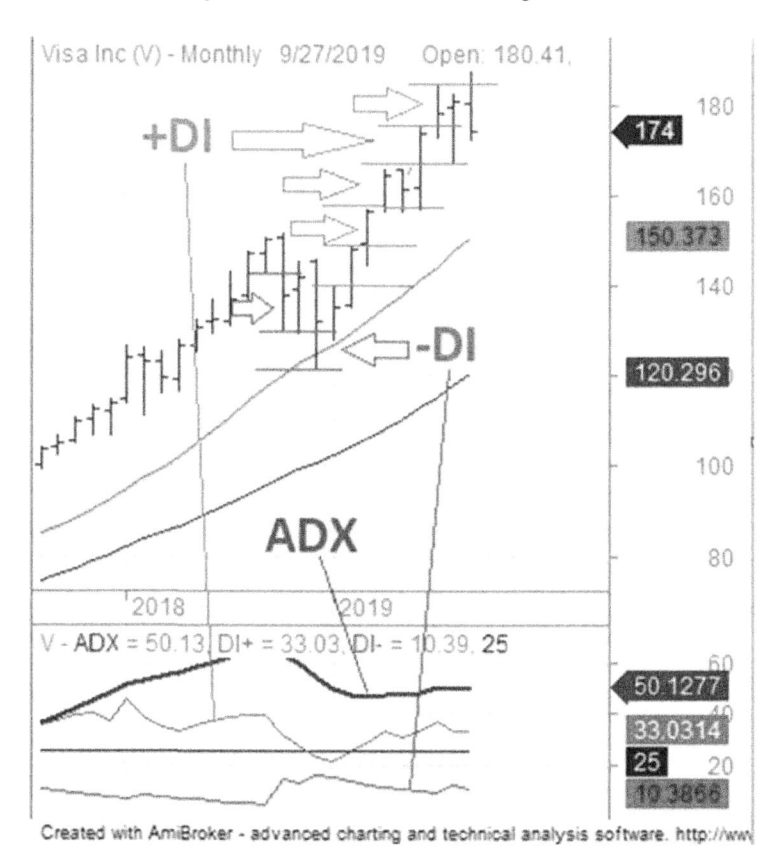

Simply put, the +DI is the strength of the buyers and the -DI is the strength of the sellers. These lines are created independent of one another. Let us start with the buying strength (+DI). The distance between the high of one bar and the bar before it shows us how much the buyers were willing to pay over and above the prior session. The arrows and lines on the chart next to the +DI show the distance between the highs. This is Positive Directional Movement (+DI or sometimes called +DM). As a stock makes higher highs, the +DI gets stronger.

On the selling side (-DI), the distance between the low of one bar and the bar before it shows us how much the sellers were willing to take the price down below its prior session. The arrows and lines on the chart next to -DI highlight the distance between the lows. As a stock makes lower lows, the -DI increases in strength.

In ADX, the side with the greatest range wins the bar and that range amount is then added to +DI or -DI. To create the lines for each, we take an average and plot them.

The ADX indicator (thick line) is created by taking the difference between these two lines and then plotting it as a moving average as well.

Charles Schaap wrote a book called ADXcellence. This is another outstanding book and it is an in-depth discussion of all aspects of ADX/DI. I recommend it for anyone who truly wants to understand this indicator and its wide variety of uses. Linda Raschke also describes her uses of ADX in some of her books, manuals and videos. Each uses this indicator in a similar fashion with a few modifications.

Schaap uses a 13 moving average of the DI lines. Most software packages use 14 by default so not a big difference there. However, he uses an 8 moving average to create ADX. Standard packages use 14. I adopted Schaap's 13, 8 settings in my analysis and interpretation of ADX. The ADX (13,8) is more responsive to changes in direction than the traditional ADX (14,14) and therefore has more peaks and valleys. This provides more insight into the strength of the last leg and becomes important in determining the strength of a pullback or rally against the trend. For our purposes, this information becomes a vital factor.

ADX is Non-Directional

The interesting and confusing fact about this indicator is that ADX is indifferent as to direction. The ADX line will rise if there is a strong trend and it does not matter whether that trend is to the upside or to the downside. It is based on the difference between the two DI lines regardless of which of the two is on top.

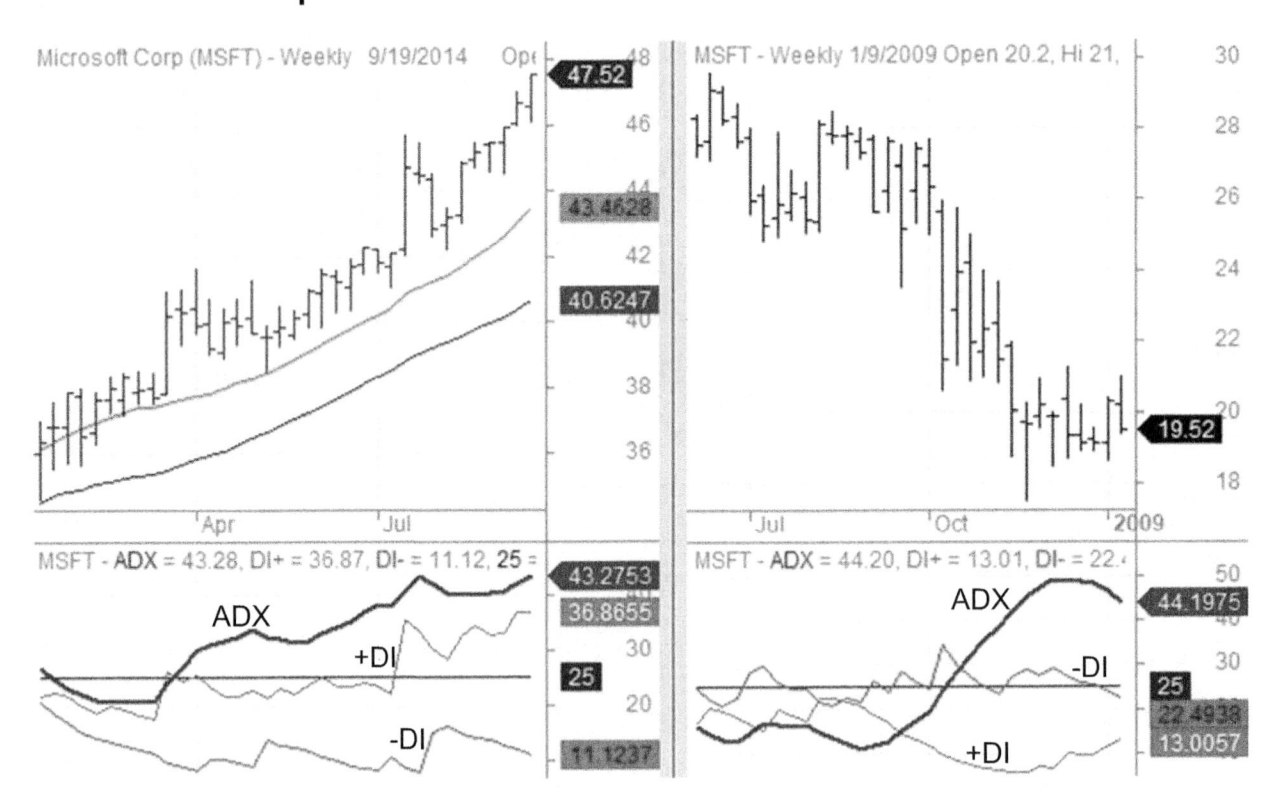

There are two weekly charts of Microsoft Corp. (MSFT) above. ADX is rising in both cases. On the left, the stock is rising and +DI is separating from -DI and this is causing the ADX to rise. On the right, -DI is separating away from +DI and the ADX line is rising.

This is a powerful indicator because you need real buying power to get it to move. Once you get used to the fact that rising = strong, ADX can be very helpful in the stock selection process. Personally, I believe this is the best indicator for determining which stock to play. If I have 2 choices where the overall price structure is the same and MA lines are generally the same, I will go to ADX to determine which is the stronger trend. Stocks with high ADX readings tend to move faster and stronger than stocks with low ADX readings.

ADX Conditions That Help in Stock Selection

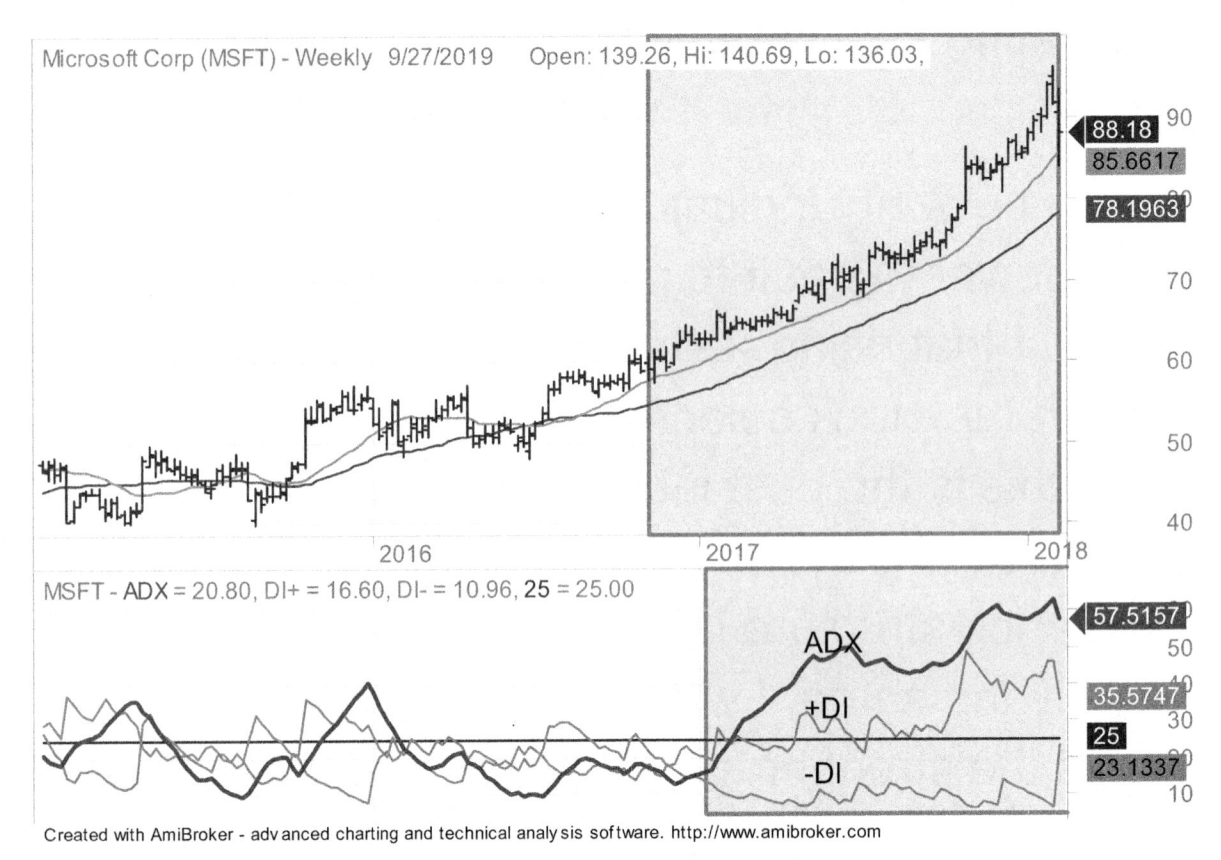

Sticking with MSFT, I have highlighted 2017. Notice how price trended starting in late 2016 with the 18-week MA line and the 40-week MA line running almost parallel for the entire year. ADX started turning up in the beginning of 2017 and rose strongly all year long. When the ADX line is strong enough to get above the 25 (line) level, the stock is in trend mode and it is okay to consider looking for entries on the lower time frame. The very strongest trends will stay above 25 throughout a pullback or correction phase. Good ADX strength is what we are looking for on the higher time frame. We want to see stocks make higher highs in price and confirm it with ADX peaks above 25. This is a great starting point if you want to use a screening tool to identify potential candidates.

Another key factor is what the stock was doing prior to the trend starting. If a stock spends a significant amount of time in a quiet basing phase or a sideways consolidation, the ADX/DI lines will all drop under 25. If this goes on long enough to form a pattern on the price chart such as an ascending triangle or a rectangle, then the likelihood is that the stock is prepping for a big move in one direction or the other.

MSFT in 2016 shows how this condition can form. The stock moved sideways for 6 months or so and the ADX lines moved down under 25. There is

some lag between price action and the ADX indicator. In fact, as I mentioned earlier, the greater the volatility of the price action, the larger the lag. Investors need to realize this fact and know that nothing is going to give an earlier signal than price itself. Every indicator is a derivative of price and therefore will usually take more time to provide the same evidence. This is the main reason I have continued to repeat myself about learning price first before moving on to indicators. When you understand price, you can anticipate. In the case of MSFT, there is no need to wait for ADX to climb above 25 before considering it as a buy because the low ADX base told you a move was coming. You can already clearly see the price has started to trend nearly 3 months before ADX crossed 25. Still, having ADX and MACD to help confirm or refute the price action are invaluable tools in your arsenal.

A few key aspects to note with ADX:

- Periods of low volatility and low ADX tend to be the precursor to big moves. However, it is best to wait for price to breakout from its range or pattern to avoid long periods of consolidation.
- Stocks with bullish price trends that have strong ADX readings are ones to monitor on pullbacks/corrections. On the higher time frame, focus on the stocks in uptrends which are confirming the higher high in price with a strong ADX reading greater than 25, preferably greater than 30.
- During the pullbacks of these strong uptrends, on the lower time frame, focus on the stocks with weak ADX (negative) readings. I will give examples to explain this in more detail.

I am going to focus on the last two aspects from above to illustrate how I incorporate ADX into my existing methodology. Keep in mind that you want to use the indicators to provide different insights rather than necessarily confirming one another. Waiting for confirmation from each indicator creates too much ambiguity to the signals and makes you question what is taking place. Not to mention, your entry will be very late waiting for every indicator to confirm.

Instead, I use the ADX to help me to determine WHICH stocks to focus on and I use the MACD to help with the timing of the trigger along with price and the MA lines as previously discussed.

Higher Time Frame Strength using ADX

I have mentioned a few times that you can identify the strength of the trend by focusing on the MA lines and their slope as well as their relationship to one another. This works fine when you are watching just a few symbols and waiting for this to develop. However, using ADX as a screening tool is very powerful. I like to look for strength on the higher time frame with this indicator. Simply screening for ADX above 25 is one way to do it. Additionally, we could look for stocks above their 18 MA line and MACD above its Signal line. However, now we are getting very specific and there will be few if any passing this type of filter. Typically, I will just screen for ADX above 25 and price above the 18 MA line for whatever time frame I am looking to invest. This screen is not a timing tool. Instead, it is a device to identify stocks which have a better chance of trending. Some of the strongest cases will have parallel MA lines on the higher time frame.

I am going to use an example on an intraday time frame which is a great situation covering all aspects of what we have already discussed. I like using intraday examples periodically to show the fractal nature of the stock market. This means that 5 1-minute segments make up a 5-minute chart and 6 5-minute segments make up a 30-minute chart and so on. When you are testing whether a method or indicator has predictive qualities, you should be able to recognize and trade signals from both short term time frames as well as long term time frames in the same manner. A chart is a chart.

The following chart is the S&P 500 tracking ETF (SPY). This is a 10-minute time frame. Notice after 12:00 EST on Oct 3rd, the 18 MA crossed above the 40 MA line and both were rising. At this stage, we have early signs that the trend has turned bullish.

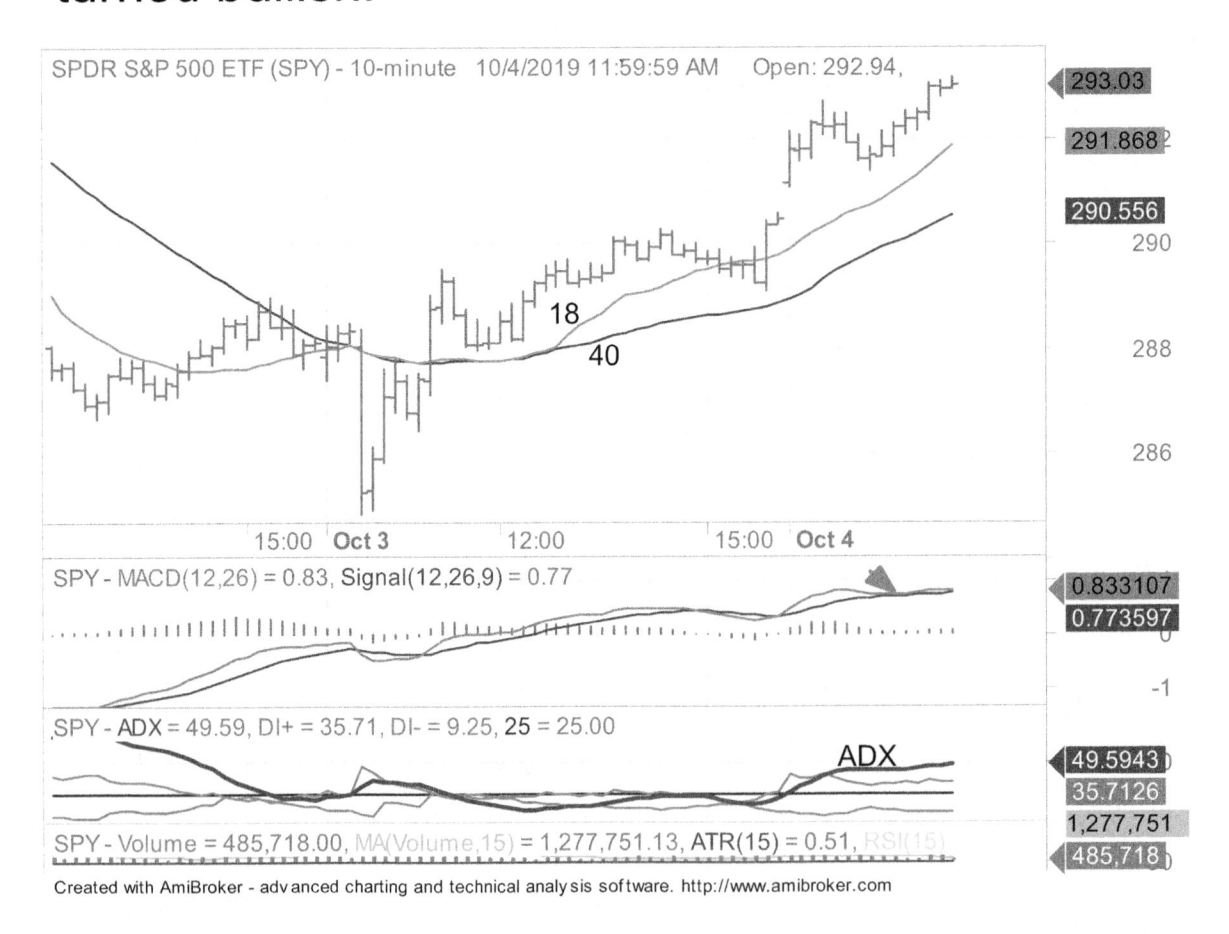

Based on the parallel nature of the MA lines, a trader could have considered buying the pullback later in the day assuming there was a qualifying trigger on the lower time frame. However, notice what happens on the Oct. 4th, a strong move off the Open caused the ADX line to cross above 25 with buyers winning the battle (+DI on top). At this point, we now have a strong trend confirmed by our ADX indicator.

Lower Time Frame – Strength of Counter Move

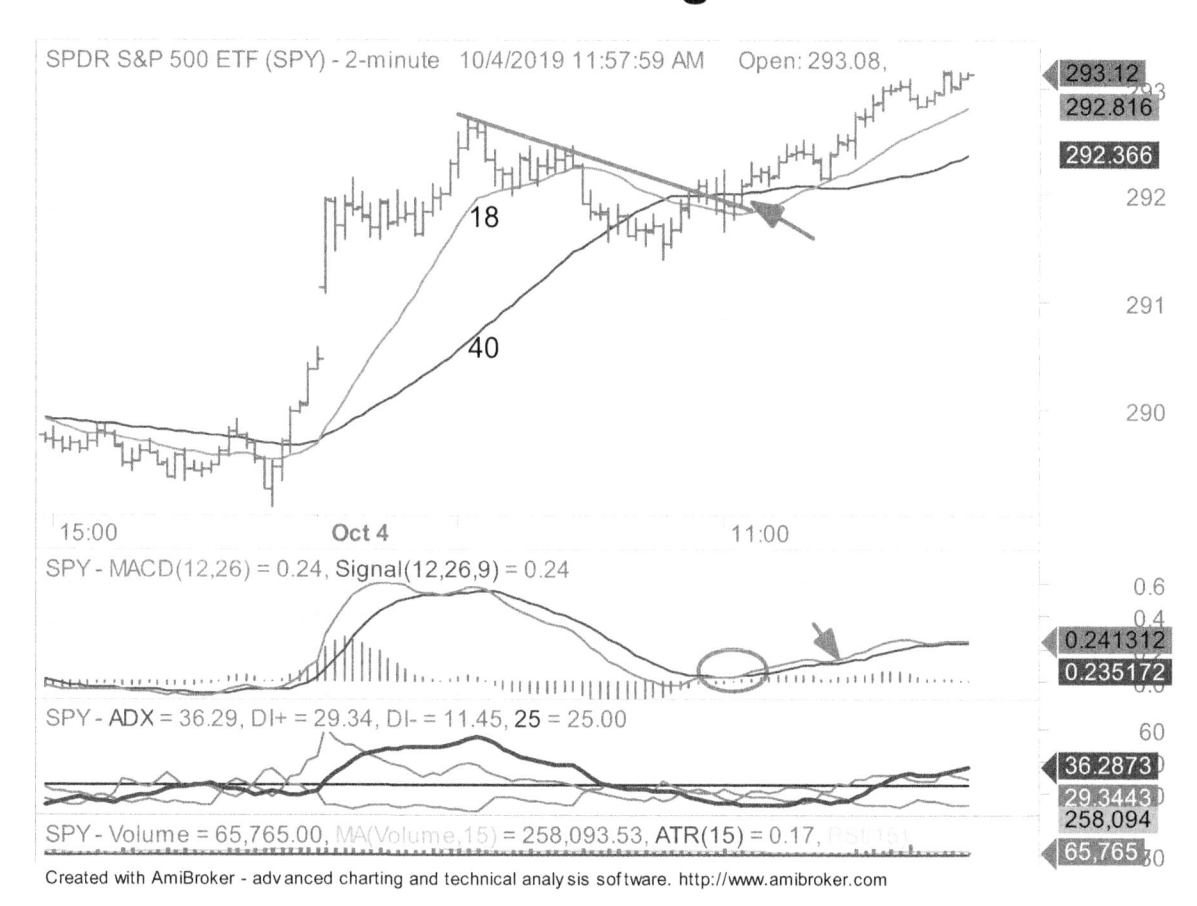

Next, we drop down to the 2-minute chart (lower time frame). Here, we use ADX differently. On this time frame, we are evaluating the pullback to see if the ADX is low. Since the decline is based on the strength of the sellers, we are looking for either a lower ADX reading than the up move before it started pulling back or low ADX (under 25) during the decline. When there is a low ADX reading on the decline, it means the -DI (in this case) is unable to get above 25 and the sellers have no real power. The 2-minute chart peaked in the morning and corrected long enough to get the 18 MA to cross down below the 40 MA line. However, -DI could never truly get above 25. Therefore, we know that the sellers are weak and that gives us a green light to go to price, the MA lines and MACD to find an entry trigger.

At approximately 11:00AM, the downtrend line was broken and the 1-2-3 started. Just after the test, we have a MA 'sell signal that fails' trigger to the upside confirmed by the MACD line crossing above its Signal line on the exact same bar. About twenty minutes later, a MACD pinch play developed and provided another opportunity to enter at the 18 MA with very low risk.

In many ways, this example covers everything we have discussed throughout this manual: Trend, change of trend, multiple time frame analysis and momentum. The majority of the two-time frame examples in this book have the same characteristics. The beauty of this illustration is that we could take the dates and times off the charts and it could easily be mistaken for a weekly/daily combination.

More ADX Examples

Morgan Stanley (MS) is another ADX example without the MACD so we can focus and understand what this indicator is telling us. The boxed area represents the same time span on both the weekly and daily time frames. Higher time frame (left) is strong confirming a strong bearish trend in 2015. Lower time frame (right) shows weak ADX on the rally confirming that the bias remains bearish.

The weekly (left) and daily (right) charts of General Mills Inc. (GIS) are another example of a strong trend on the higher time frame and a weaker trend during the decline in 2013. On the right chart (daily – lower time frame), the +DI was strong enough to climb above 25 and get the ADX line to do the same. However, compare the peak of the ADX on the decline (arrow) to the big peak made by the buyers before the correction (horizontal line). It becomes crystal clear that the buyers had more strength and as a result we continue to look at this stock as a potential buy candidate referring to trend, MA lines and MACD to refine entry.

The final ADX example is the weekly and daily of Twitter Inc. (TWTR) in 2018. In this example, the ADX was very strong on the weekly chart. During the correction, the ADX reading only dropped to around 40. That is powerful. On the right, the daily chart shows the decline was also steep, dropping around 10 points in about two weeks. The ADX reading on the selloff reached 40 but was still well below the reading from the buyers which peaked near 60 in March. While we still have an upward bias here, it is important to point out that when the sellers have some strength like this, the trigger signal is likely to take longer to develop.

Use ADX to help with stock selection. Strong ADX patterns on the higher time frame will keep you focused on stocks with the strongest trends which will move faster and further.

Also, during corrections on the lower time frame, be mindful of the severity of the counter trend move and compare the strength of this counter move to the strength of the move before the correction started.

Adding ADX to your analysis will improve your accuracy and will increase the size of your average win.

Trading Tactics

There are a few different ways to use the methods described in this manual. First, you could apply the timing methods in a stock that you are interested in fundamentally. The benefit to using this approach along with the fundamentals is that it will help to prevent you from buying a good stock at the wrong time. I have been trading and investing for a long time. No matter how much confidence you have when you decide to buy a stock, if it starts moving against you immediately, it will test your conviction. It is better to have a plan in place and an understanding of where you are in the main trend of the stock and the methods to take advantage of that. There is only one real tactic after entry that I would recommend for the fundamental based buy: Do not hold the stock if it clearly breaks its 18-month MA line. A clear break of this key MA line would make you vulnerable to potentially significant downside risk and it is worth standing aside and reassessing.

The second approach to using these methods is to buy with the entry signals described as a stand-alone system. While I recommend doing some form of screen on market cap and trading volume, you can take the setups defined and apply them to monthly/weekly trades or weekly/daily combinations. If you are going to trade off the technical patterns alone, I recommend employing some trading tactics to protect yourself and improve your overall performance over time.

I have shown entry points but have purposely left out stops, trailing stops and targets up until this point. Managing a position after entering can be an entire book on its own. However, there are a few tactics I would suggest that you could employ which reduce risk and still provide you with the opportunity for a big win. It is important to realize that investing using technical analysis without fundamental analysis can be done but you must understand that you do not know where your best wins will come from. This means you need a consistent method applied across the board to all trades/investments and then it turns into a numbers game over time.

As far as stops are concerned, I would recommend putting your initial stop below the last bottom on a buy setup. So, if your trigger is crossing above the

40-weekly MA line, go back and look for the last bottom. Preferably, it will be a higher bottom, but either way that should be your initial stop point. I will show examples of this in the next section.

I have found the best setups take place when you go inside the 18/40 zone and out and then trigger above the 40-MA line. This creates the higher bottom and will often look like the change of trend sequence described earlier in the text. Once the stop is in place, calculate the difference between the stop and your entry point. Add this number to your entry point and look to exit one-quarter to one-third of your position at this level. In addition, raise the stop on the remaining shares to breakeven. At this point, you will have booked some small profits and still have at least two-thirds of your position to take advantage of further upside in the trend. If it reaches two or three times what you risk, consider scaling out further. The stop can then be raised using either the 18 MA on the entry time frame or the 40 MA depending on your risk tolerance and how much upside appears to be in place on the higher time frame. If you took one-third profit at one-times, two-times and three-times your initial risk, your overall average profit would be 2:1. This is a good enough amount of profit-relative-to-risk to be successful over time, assuming you are strict about the trend of the higher time frame and your entries are good. Figure out the profit scaling levels that make sense to you and handle each investment the same way. Consistency in the management will be an important key to your success.

Trading Plan for 2 Time Frame MACD Pinch

The following strategy is a good starting point for someone who would like to get more proficient at trading in multiple time frames. For this strategy, we are going to use more simplified trading tactics than I laid out in the previous section. I use a 3:1 reward to risk target level in this approach.

In most cases, these signals will provide low risk entry points in the direction of the higher time frame trend. Additionally, based on the criteria, it will ensure that the higher time frame is not too overbought or extended from support or resistance. This helps to reduce pullback risk. Pullback risk is defined as having too much distance between price and the 18 MA line on the higher time frame. The further price gets away from this line, the higher the risk of a retracement back to it. This plan is designed to reduce this type of risk.

I recommend using this plan on a handful of stocks and implementing all the qualifying trades until you have made 20-25 trades. You will better see how two time frames work together and you can then adjust the plan to suit your needs by allowing the trigger on the lower time frame to be a little more flexible depending on the price structure.

This strategy can be used with any two time frames- monthly/weekly, weekly/daily, daily/60 minute, 60 minute/10 minute, and 30 minute/5 minute. Initially, examples of daily/60 minute will be used to find swing trades lasting 1-5 days.

Using a $100,000 account, each trade will risk $500 or .5% of the total account. Although this is on the small side, it gives the opportunity to take lots of different setups. Also, this reduces the risk of adverse morning gaps. If using the weekly/daily combo, $1000 or 1% is an acceptable number since trades take longer to develop on these time frames. You can risk more on a monthly/weekly version of this trade but never risk more than 2% of equity on any signal investment.

The total portfolio risk at any time should never be more than 5%. So, using a $100,000 account, total risk should never exceed $5000 at any given time. Essentially, this limits trading to 10 open trades at a time (using .5%). In addition, this 5% rules applies to the entire month. Therefore, if you have closed losses for the month of $2500, then the maximum allowed positions would then be 5. In other words, if total losses for the month ever exceed $5000, then stop trading for the month.

Limit trading ideas to 3 per sector. This helps diversify some of the risk as well. This prevents owning 10 energy stocks at the same time. In many ways, that is like having one big position.

Start with the Daily chart for the Daily/60 min setup:

1-the MACD must have crossed above the Signal line.

2- the price should be above or very close to the 18-day ma.

3- once the cross is in place, we are looking for a 2 bar pullback. That is, 2 consecutive lower highs (it is okay if one of the highs is equal rather than lower.) I also prefer to see price pullback near the 18 MA but this is not necessary. In addition, 3, 4 or 5 bar pullbacks also qualify as long as the MACD holds above its Signal line.

4- after the 2 bar pullback we are waiting for the 1st day where the previous high is violated. This violation must occur before the MACD moves back below the Signal line.

5- Once we have an operative buy signal on the daily chart, we go to the 60 min chart.

6- now we look for the next identical setup on the 60 min chart. MACD is above Signal line and price is above its 18-day ma.

7- after a 2 bar pullback on the 60 min chart, we then place a buy stop order above the previous bar's high. For each bar, continue to place a buy stop above the previous bar's high until your order is filled or the 60 min MACD crosses back below its Signal line. If the Signal line is violated, cancel the order to buy. It is possible for the MACD to go below the Signal line by a small degree and then turn back above. In these cases, it is best not to have a resting buy stop order in place. Instead, watch as the previous high is exceeded and see if the MACD is above its Signal line. If it is, then it is okay to enter a buy order.

Here is a chart example of this setup:

Daily chart - higher time frame:

1 – MACD line above Signal line

2- price above 18-day ma.

3- 2 bar pullback

4- price trades above previous bar's high

Once we have identified this pattern on the daily chart, we then drop down to the 60 min chart and look for the same setup to occur. Sometimes the pattern will occur simultaneously and other times it will come a day or two later. Just be patient and wait for the signal on the 60 min for the highest probability setup. If the signal takes place on the daily chart and moves higher for 2 full days without giving the trigger on the lower time frame, then disregard the trade and look for another stock. The goal is to reduce pullback risk on the higher time frame, so we do not want to buy after three days up.

The following page shows a 60 min chart of the same time period just discussed:

60 minute chart - lower time frame:

On this chart we see the stock gapped up the day following the signal on the daily chart. The stock then spent the following couple of hours making lower highs until the high of an hourly bar was violated. Notice how the MACD line and Signal line were both rising during this pullback phase. Also, I like to see the two lines coming together. In many cases they pinch. This is the case on the daily chart. The 2 bar pullback caused the MACD line to pinch into the signal line. When this occurs while price is pulling back to the 18 MA, there is typically a good trade setup developing.

Now, let's look at how to handle the trade from a trade management standpoint.

We know we are risking $500. In order to find the number of shares to buy, we must now find the low price of the pullback on the 60 min chart. In this case, the low is $11.30. Our entry is above the last lower high which is $11.52. So, our entry is $11.53, and stop is $11.29. (If you would like, you can add .05 to entry and stop to reduce false moves. However, this system enters and exits on .01-02 cents violations. Our risk on the trade (not including slippage) is $.24. Taking the $500 and dividing by the .24 risk, we know we can buy 2082 shares. We round that to 2000.

We buy 2000 shares with a buy stop at $11.53. At this point, the stop is put in place at $11.29. Then, take the .24 and multiply it by 3. This gives us $.72. Add this amount to the entry price and put a limit in at $12.25 (See chart below.) Use OCA (order cancels all) if possible so if one order is hit, the other is cancelled. At this point, let the trade play out. One more calculation is necessary. Divide $.72 by 2 and we get $.36. Add this amount to the entry.

When this level is hit, move the stop loss order from the low to breakeven. In this case, when the stock reaches $11.89, we move our stop to breakeven at $11.53. That is it.

Otherwise, let these trades play out. With a reward-to-risk ratio of 3-1, you only need to be right 3 times out of 10 to make money. At 4 times out of 10, you are not only making money, your profit factor is 2.00 which is a level that can compound money quickly. If you are right 50% of the time, the numbers are exceptional.

In this example, the stock reached $12.25 the following day. Our $500 risk turned into a $1500 profit. We take the money and run. We don't need to milk every position to make good money in the market.

Realize that just because a trade qualifies on a daily chart does not mean it will give an entry signal. It is important to watch the 60 min chart for the final trigger. The following chart shows the daily qualifying signals that developed during the upmove in the Williams Co. (WMB). The circles are where all 4 pattern criteria are met on the daily chart. There were 5 signals including the one we have already covered in detail. By using the 60 min to refine entry and lower risk, there will be times that you will miss moves. This needs to be accepted as a part of the plan. Using the 60 min entry, the results of the 5 trades were as follows: 1st- win -$1500 (already discussed), 2nd- breakeven-$0, 3rd-loss-$500, 4th-win-$1500, 5th-win-$1500. Totals- 3 wins = $4500, 1 loss = $500, 1 breakeven = $0. Total profit = $4000 and that is a profit factor of 9 (Total Profits/Total Losses). This was a good run. I would expect wins and losses to run about equal or just slightly in favor of the losses with about 25% of the trades ending in breakeven.

[Chart: WMB - Daily 6/12/2009 9:30:00 AM Open 17.47, Hi 17.57, Lo 17.21, Close 17.36 (-1.5%)]

This dual time frame MACD pinch pattern happens all the time in both directions and in all time frames. Like any approach in the stock market, the key to success is patience and discipline. As I stated at the beginning of this book, swing trading will go through good and bad phases. It is critical to recognize the general market volatility is affecting your trading. If it is a time when economic uncertainty clouds the picture, then each new economic number can cause gaps in different directions. This is not an ideal market environment for swing trading.

The chart above shows a weekly chart of SAIA Inc. (SAIA). The arrow shows a setup on the weekly chart where all criteria are met except price is not above 18-MA. In these cases, I believe it is okay to go to the daily chart and watch for a signal. My reasoning is that the MACD is clearly showing improving momentum characteristics and price has pulled back which are the 2 most important criteria for the higher time frame. So, we have the wind at our backs, and we don't have pullback risk from the higher time frame. However, it is critical that the stock be above the 18 MA on the entry time frame.

In this case, the daily chart can only qualify for entry if all 4 criteria are met.

The daily chart of SAIA triggered 2 weeks after the weekly setup was in place. Again, this shows the need to be patient and organized. If using this approach for longer term swing trades, it makes sense to keep a list of stocks which have met the requirement on the weekly chart and then monitor them closely on the daily chart each day.

One note about gaps. This is more important when using the daily/60 min combo. If a buy signal is triggered via a gap, my suggestion is to either pass on the trade or wait for a second entry. This would mean we would wait for the gap to be filled and then the next time through the original entry point, the stock can be purchased. This assumes that MACD is still holding its signal line when second entry is triggered.

The weekly chart of Johnson Controls Inc. (JCI) shows a different setup than what we have described. Instead of price being above 18-MA and MACD holding above the Signal line, price makes a new low and MACD makes a higher low. In this chart, the price of JCI makes a low in November 2008 and then another low in March 2009.

However, the MACD makes a low in November 2008 but does not make a new low in March 2009. This is the bullish momentum divergence pattern described earlier in the book.

When this occurs, if criteria 3 and 4 take place on this weekly chart, we can then turn to our daily chart to look for all 4 criteria to be met. I still consider this a 2-time frame MACD pinch, even though the pinch is only occurring on the entry time frame. I like to see the weekly MACD cross its Signal line before a daily trigger takes place. Again, the goal of the higher time frame is to tell us which direction has the momentum and to make sure we do not have a large pullback risk. Again, pullback risk refers to when price has carried a little too far from its moving average and there is a risk of correction back to it. The 18 MA acts as a leash and when price moves away from it, the MA line pulls it back closer to it.

The following chart shows the daily chart of JCI a few weeks after the divergence occurs on the weekly chart. Notice the nice separation price gets from the 18 MA before pulling back to it. Also, the MACD makes a nice soft pinch during the 3 bar pullback. To clarify, a 2 bar pullback is the minimum requirement, but it is not necessary. Some of the best trade setups will come from 3, 4 and 5 bar pullbacks. What you will notice is that if there is good separation on the move up in price, then the pullback can be 3-5 bars and the MACD will still hold its Signal line. But, if the cross is mild, then the pullback must be mild as well.

My favorite patterns are when the price and MACD show strong movement and separation before starting the pullback phase. Notice that after the trade triggered, there was a pause day before price moved higher to reach the upside target. That pause day was the setup developing on the 60 min chart.

In the case of a higher time frame divergence, when we move to the lower time frame there is an additional factor that needs to be determined. Since momentum divergence only promises a retracement back to resistance, we need to calculate the distance from the lower time frame signal to the higher time frame MA line. If you enter on the lower time frame, there needs to be enough room to the higher time frame resistance to allow you to move your stop to a breakeven. In other words, the minimum requirement would be 1.5 times your risk to reach either the 18 MA or the 40 MA line on the higher time frame. In this case, the 18 MA on the higher time frame was above the 3 to 1 target which is ideal.

There is nothing stopping you from dropping down a third time frame to lower the risk on the trade. Keep in mind, each time you drop a time frame, you increase the odds of being stopped out. In some cases, this will happen and then the daily time frame will continue to move higher without being stopped out. My suggestion is that if you are going to drop down to a third time frame, continue to use the second time frame for your target. To clarify. When the weekly pattern meets the 4 criteria or is a momentum divergence, then move down to the daily chart. When all 4 criteria are met, look for the same pattern on the 60-minute chart. However, for this type of trade, we set the stop on the 60-minute chart and the target on the daily chart. This will increase the reward to risk equation in your favor. In some cases, from 3-1 to 5-1 or 7-1.

I am going to finish this chapter by giving more examples of this pattern in different time frames.

Daily chart – higher time frame:

Here is an example of a short sale using the Daily/60 min combination. There was nice separation of the MACD line versus its Signal line on this daily chart and that is a sign of strength in the move.

60 min triggered the same day, but later in the afternoon. The target was $16.34 which was reached in the morning of day 3. There was not a pinch on the daily chart but that is okay since the momentum was clearly down. We are not trying to hit home runs here. Just keep finding dual time frame patterns and bank them. I can almost guarantee that you will leave money on the table trading in this manner. However, there will also be times when you bank profits just in time, literally by pennies before a reversal. Consistency comes through strict money management and sector diversification.

Daily chart – higher time frame:

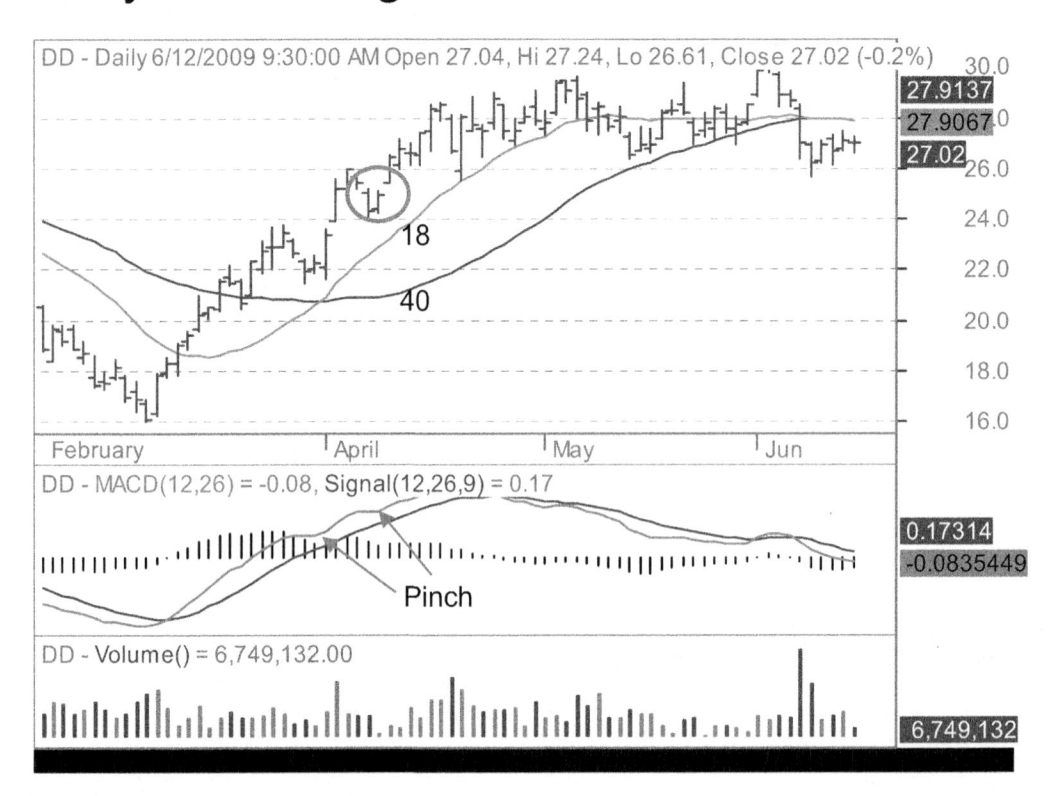

Circled area shows the second signal on the daily chart. I will typically only do the first two signals on the higher time frame. Those are the highest probability patterns for this type of setup.

60-minute chart – lower time frame:

For the trigger time frame, first entry was breakeven. Second attempt triggered on day 2 and hit the target before the end of day. It takes great discipline to go right back into the same stock after being stopped out, but this is what is necessary to be successful in the markets at times.

30-minute chart – higher time frame:

Here is a 30 min/5 min combination. Stock gapped up in the morning but still qualified on 30 min time frame. On a gap up on the higher time frame, it is critical that price does not keep running before the lower time frame trigger.

5-minute chart – lower time frame:

The 5-minute chart setup after about 30 to 40 minutes of trading and did not carry that far away from the original gap up level. Then, it hit the target about an hour later. Be patient and wait for a qualifying signal. Sometimes you will miss the move altogether, but you will be more consistent and profitable if you stay disciplined and wait for the proper time to strike.

60-minute chart – higher time frame:

Here is another example of how this approach can be used on the short side. Here is a short using the 60 min and 10 min. Above, we see the 60 min chart triggered on the gap down at the open.

10-minute chart – lower time frame:

I left the circled area from 60 min on the 10 min chart so we can see the timing of the trigger. Notice how the trigger took place before a big extended move. That is important when the higher time frame qualifies via a gap. Target was hit by .04 before turning up.

30-minute chart – higher time frame:

Here is an example of a losing trade which we can learn from. Above is a 30 min chart which shows a buy trigger. Notice how at the time of trigger, the 18 MA was still falling and there was no pinch on MACD. Nevertheless, the stock qualifies. Then, below the inner circle shows the criteria being met on the 5 min chart. However, the 2 bar pullback was not much of a pullback at all and there was no pinch on MACD.

5-minute chart – lower time frame:

There is no trading plan that will be perfect. Every plan will have losing trades. You can improve your accuracy with this approach by looking for the obvious setups which clearly qualify and have supporting evidence from price structure (1-2-3) and MA line signals. Nonetheless, losing trades will happen. The money management side of this system will be the key to your success. As much as possible, keep your losses to 1:1 on the losing trades. There will likely be a little slippage on your trades and that is okay. And, every so often there will be a gap which causes you to lose 2 times (or more) what you risked. This is a part of trading and must be accepted. You will also have some gaps in your favor which allow you to gain 4 or 5 to 1 on your money. Remain disciplined and be picky with this setup. This system provides plenty of trades so there is no reason to force sub-optimal patterns.

Why Trading is So Difficult – the Math

Trader's equation = (Win Rate x Avg Win Size) – (Loss Rate x Avg Loss Size).

Using the example in the prior section, let us study the trader's equation and its implications from a psychological standpoint. If you are right 40% of the time and you win 3 times what you risk in a trade on average. Then 60% of the time you are wrong but you keep your losses at 1 times your original risk. After 20 trades where your risk amount is $500, you would have 8 wins and 12 losses. Your wins would each make $1500 and your losses would be $500. So, (8 x 1500) – (12 x 500) = $12,000 - $6,000 = $6000 profit. Risking $500 per trade after 20 trades, the total risk is $10,000. Your profit is $6000. This equates to .60 for every $1 risked. If you could successfully invest this way and find a decent number of trades to make, your account would grow nicely over time. Why is this so difficult to achieve?

The reality is that being right 40% of the time is very achievable. Using the methods described, winning 3 times what you risk is also achievable. The problem lies in statistics and winning/losing streaks and their consequences on your psyche.

For a moment, I am going to improve the numbers and suggest that you can be right 50% of the time. Believe me, I know you are thinking that 40% is not very good. Maybe you think 50% is not very good either. Once you see the power of the numbers, you will realize that the size of the average win is very important to your success. Winning more often makes you feel good but if you only win half of what you risk on average, then even a win ratio of 70-80% will be difficult to make money.

It is all in the numbers. If you want a higher win ratio, then reduce the goal amount of the average win. For instance, instead of 3 x 1, try for 2 x 1. In this scenario, 50% wins = $10,000 (10 x 1000) in gains and the losses equate to $5000 (10 x 500) netting a gain of $5000 after 20 trades. While the final amount of money is less, I will show how it is more realistic to achieve this scenario than the 40%, 3 to 1 scenario.

Streaks

Take note of the information below. I used a streak calculator to show in a 100 trade sample with a 50%-win rate/loss rate, that the chance of losing 5 times in a row is more than 80%. These numbers have significant implications with respect to pulling the trigger when your methodology provides you a buy signal. Will you take the signal each and every time? Or will you pick and choose when you feel good about it?

Streak Calculator

Series Length:	100
Streak Length:	5
Loss Probability:	50.000%
Streak Probability:	80.453%

Calculate

The reality is that the average investor will stop after 3-4 losses in a row. They will assume, at this point, that the methodology they are using does not work. However, this is just not the case. To be successful, you will need to be able to trade through a losing streak and get to the other side.

Below, I have changed the numbers in the streak calculator. I have upped the number of trades to 200 and changed the win rate to 70% (so loss probability is now 30%). There is still a 68% chance of losing 4 times in a row after 200 trades.

Streak Calculator

Series Length:	200
Streak Length:	4
Loss Probability:	30.000%
Streak Probability:	68.086%

Calculate

So, no matter how good you are at picking stocks and timing your entries, you need to understand the psychological struggles with losing streaks and have the ability to continue to follow your rules after 3-5 losses in a row. Overcoming this roadblock to success, will likely help you to achieve more consistent results than learning more about technical analysis.

Mark Douglas wrote a book called "Trading in the Zone" and discusses everything related to the psychological side of trading. It is a must read if you are truly interested in getting better at investing.

More Examples to Study

The following charts show more examples of the goal to multiple time frame investing: Finding two consecutive time frames with bullish conditions and look to ride the trend on the lower time frame with the wind at your back from the higher time frame. Quite often, the best buying chances develop following a pullback or correction on the higher time frame. I boxed one of these pullbacks on both the monthly and weekly charts below. These boxes represent where the monthly is in an uptrend (or downtrend) and where the weekly chart is turning back into uptrend (downtrend) mode again after being in a bearish (bullish) trend. As I have stated several times, this method will work for any two consecutive time frames. You should be able to identify a trend on a specific time frame and then see a pullback. Then, go to the lower time frame and find the entry trigger.

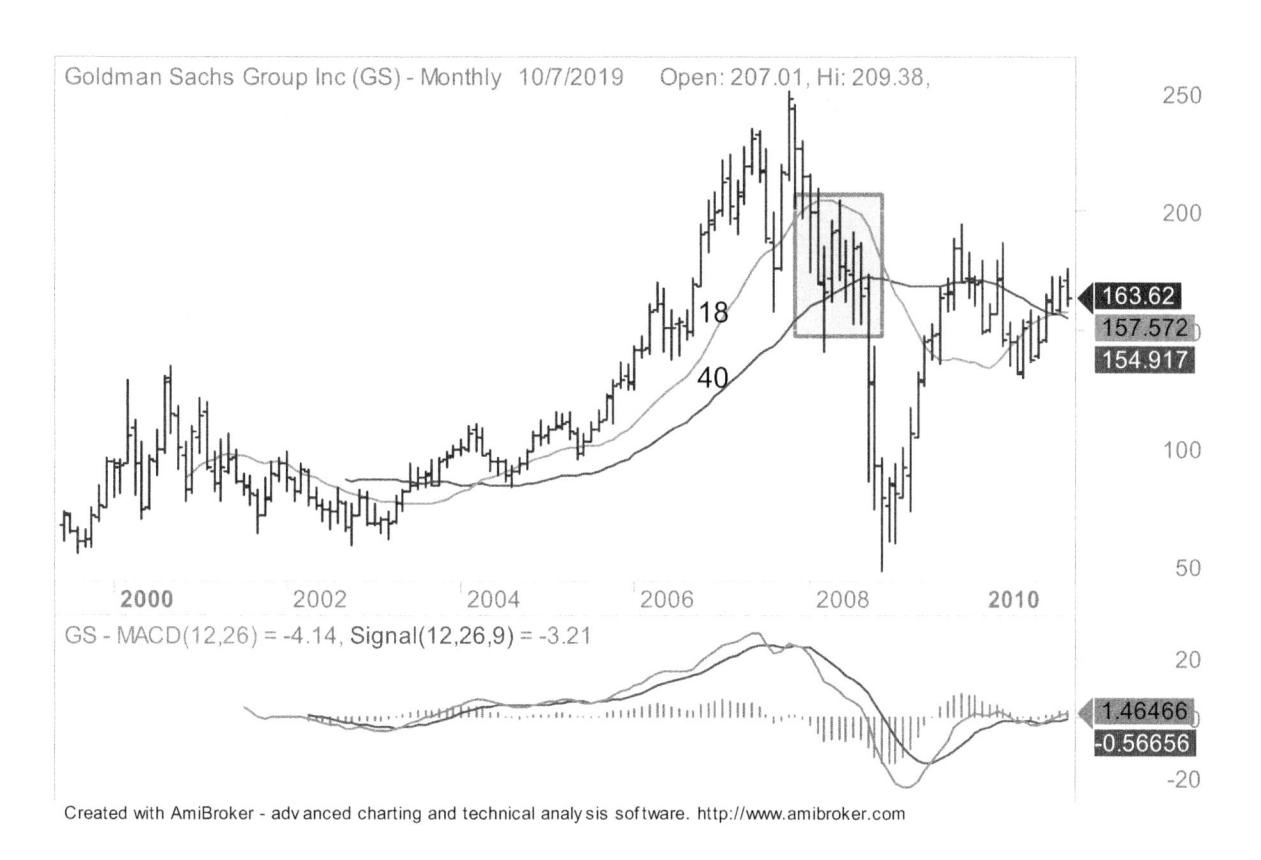

GS – monthly chart fails at the 18 MA in early 2008. Weekly MA lines gave a classis sell signal but had lots of volatility. MACD sell helped with timing.

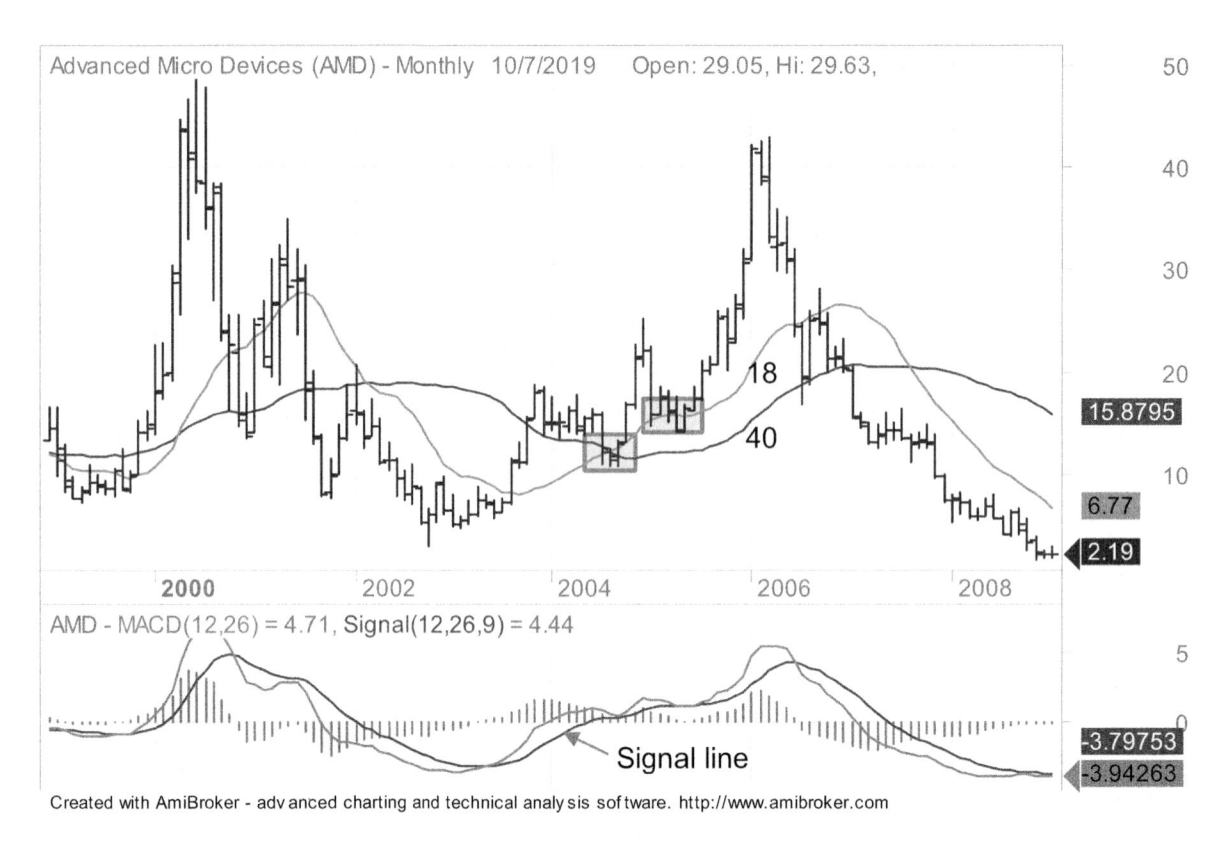

AMD – two nice pullbacks to 18-month MA line in 2004-2005. On weekly below, trigger to enter was aided by MACD crossing the Signal line. Second also had a nice pinch play buy.

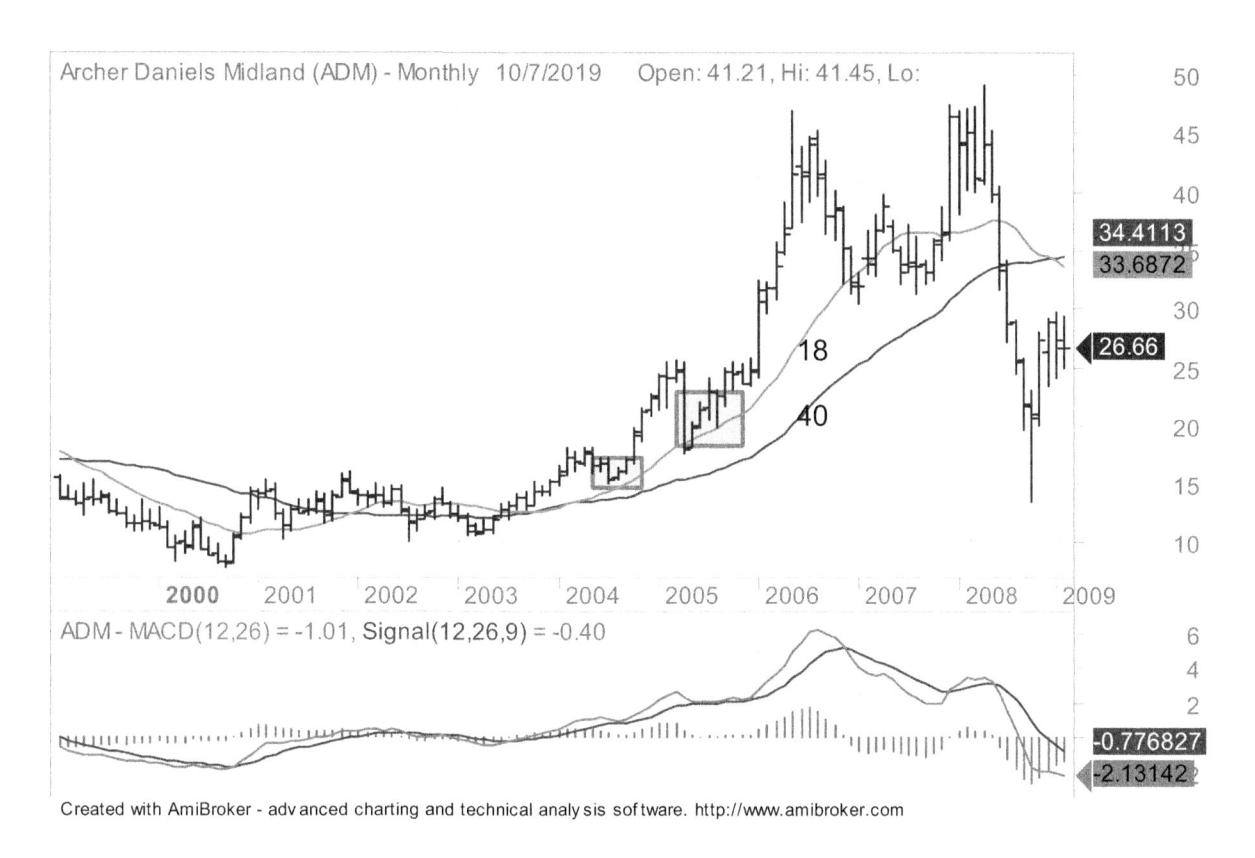

ADM – one signal in 2004 and another in 2005. First entry below was zero line reversal and 1-2-3 change in trend. Second signal was a pinch play on first pullback.

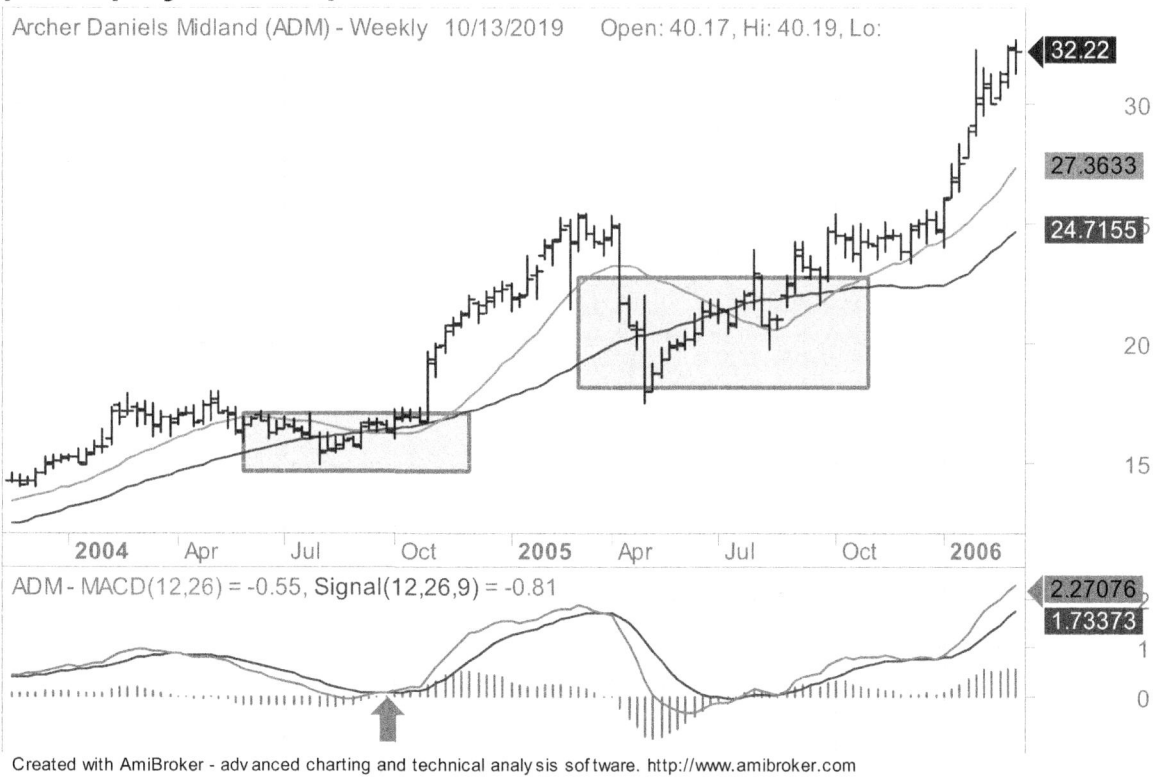

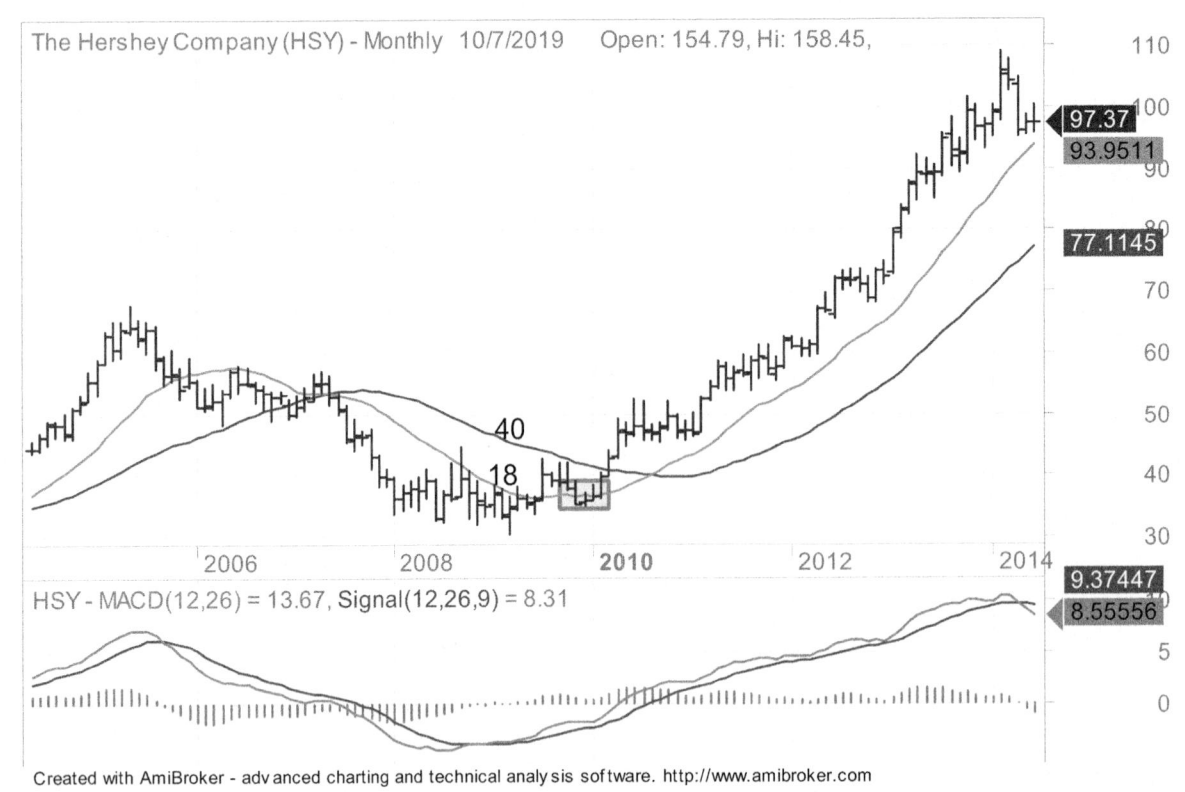

HSY – 40 to 18 bounce on monthly chart after long decline signals the long term trend is changing to positive. Trigger is 'sell signal that fails' and MACD crossover.

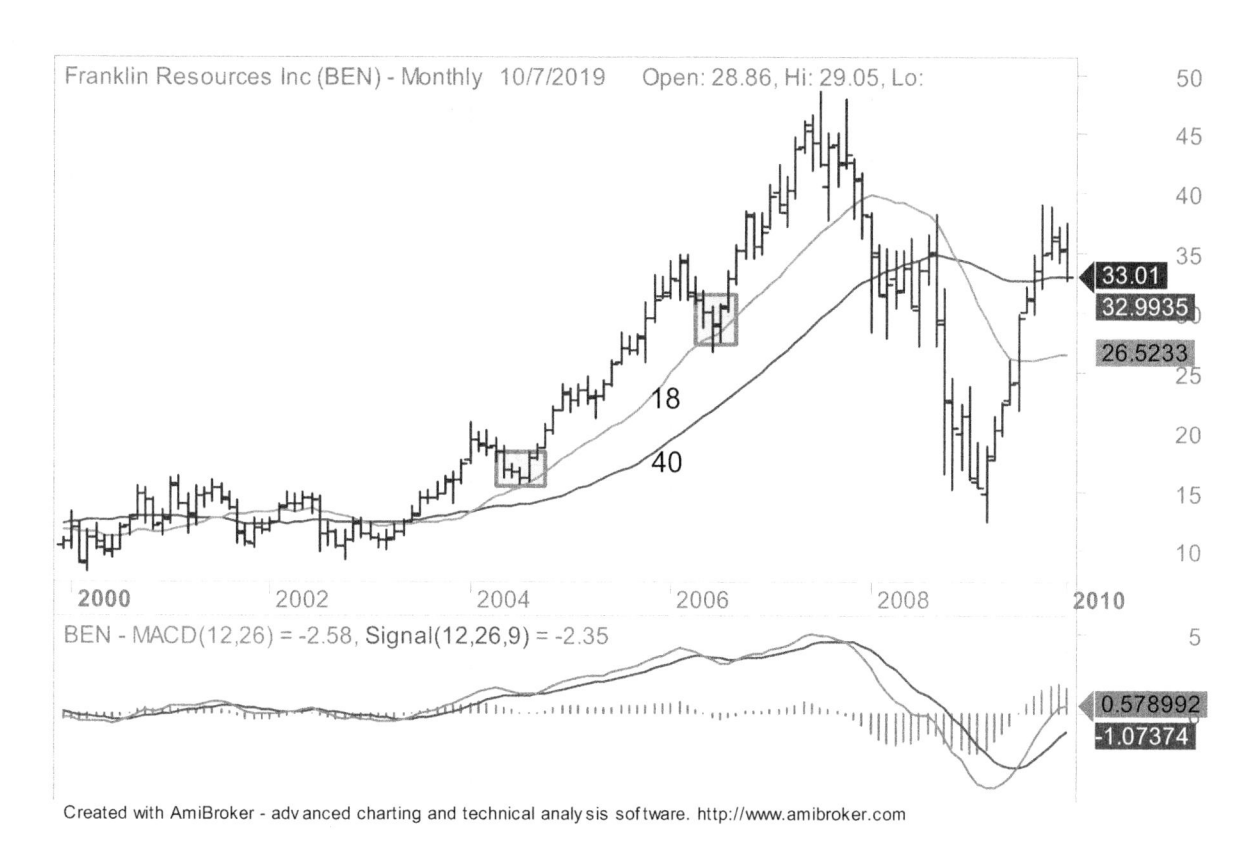

BEN – First pullback in new uptrend in 2004. Then strong parallel lines in 2005 on monthly. Weekly provided similar entry triggers as price crossed the 40 MA and MACD lines confirmed.

The charts on the previous pages show numerous examples of the two-time frame patterns that have been discussed throughout the text. Go back through these examples several times. The red boxes are aligned on the two different time frames to show where the setups take place. Notice that first chart is the monthly chart and shows the direction of the trend and the second chart is the weekly which depicts the optimum entry point using one of the signals previously mentioned in this text. Most of the entry patterns shown on the weekly charts are the 'classic sell signal that fails.' The bullish version of this pattern is described on page 20. Also, notice that in some cases the 18-month MA line is just starting to turn and in others this MA line has been rising for some time. These are important distinctions that help to provide a better idea of where the stock is in relation to its long-term trend.

After studying the charts, look through your holdings for examples of these two-time frame patterns in any two time frames. Finding and studying numerous examples will help with identifying these patterns as they come along in real time.

Conclusion

This manual should help investors to understand how to incorporate multiple time frames into their approach. The tactics laid out in this text can easily be combined with a fundamental methodology to help improve the timing of entry and exits. I have been using many of these techniques for the past 30 years to help professional investors make more timely entries and exits with their buy and sell decisions. This process took a long time to develop and may not be obvious to you after reading this manual once. It is important to go through the charts several times and then look for examples taking place right now to help ingrain the patterns. Many of the charts from this manual are dated. This is important to note because this method has withstood the test of time. I wanted to show how the charts from several years ago look the same as today.

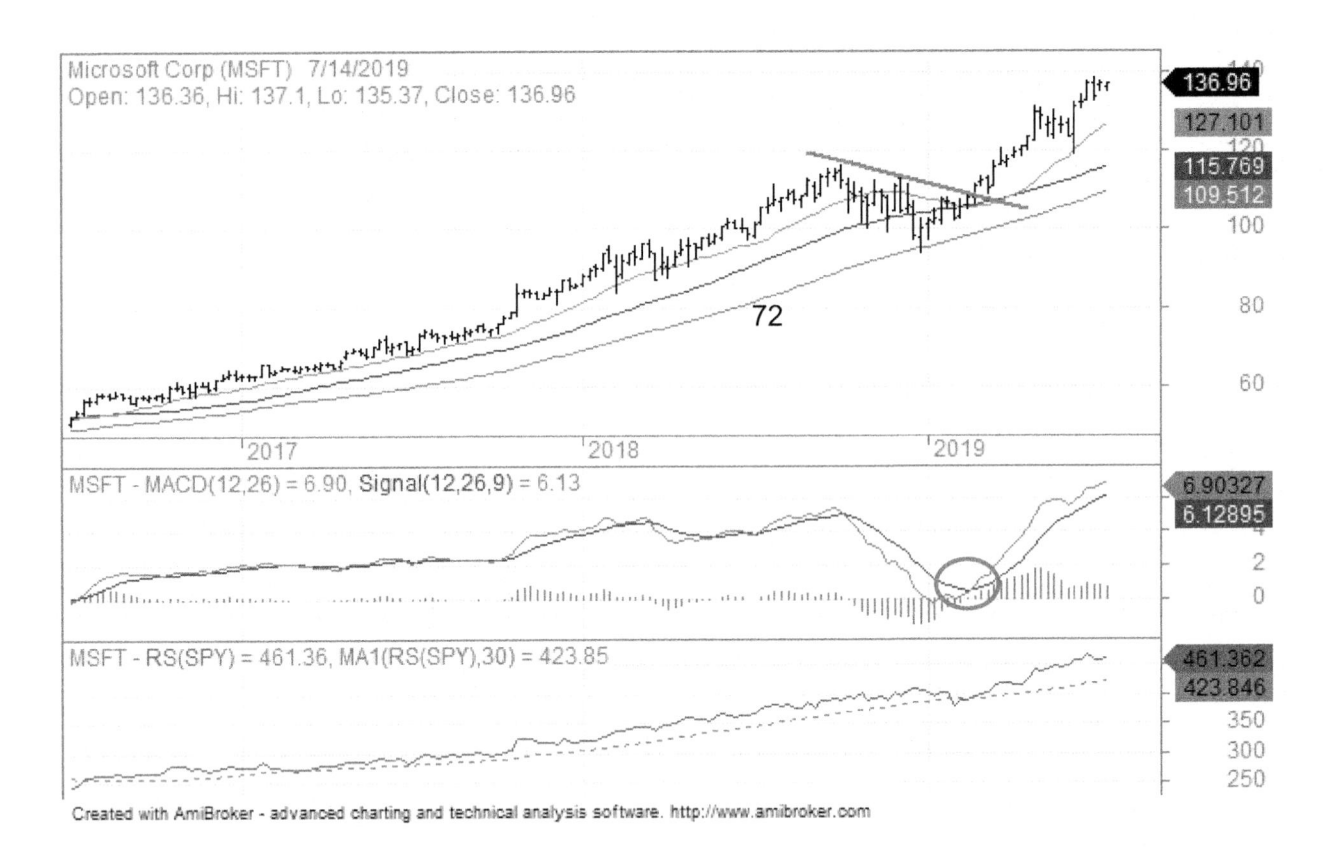

I will end this text with an example from this year (2019). Here is a weekly chart of Microsoft (MSFT). There is an 18-week MA and a 40-week MA line as well as a 72-week MA. The 72-week MA line is very close to the 18-month MA line in length and works well as a substitute on the weekly chart if you do not have the ability to look at two charts at the same time. In early 2019, after a 6-month correction, the 18-week MA corrected back and touched the 40-week MA line. As previously discussed, the trigger for this type of pattern is a break of the downtrend line and is confirmed by the MACD cross of the Signal line following a zero line reversal. This example illustrates how the methodology continues to provide excellent opportunities in today's market to improve your timing using multiple time frames combined with trend analysis.

You only need one method or tactic that happens consistently in the market to be successful over time. Learn the few approaches discussed in this book and become proficient at recognizing them. Employ them with a consistent money management approach and your odds of success are good.

Printed in Great Britain
by Amazon